Rich Little Piggy

Build a Financial House of BRICK!

David W. Robbins

Copyright © 2014 David W. Robbins

All rights reserved.

ISBN-10: 1505624274
ISBN-13: 978-1505624274

DEDICATION

This book is dedicated to the hard-working people who pound it out every day. To the men and women who do the *right* thing, not the *easy* thing.

To the Soldiers, Sailors, Airmen, and Marines who risk their lives to defend ours. Freedom is not free and they have paid the price.

To the first responders who place our safety above theirs - the policemen, firemen, and emergency medical staff. Our 911. Our rescuers.

To the teachers in the classroom and the servers on the line. To the workers in the field and the laborers everywhere. For the long hours and aching muscles. They get it done.

To the mothers and fathers. Our role models. Our heroes. They are inspiration and hope.

To those in the shadows. To those without a voice.

Let your day begin.

Dear Prospective Piggy,

On the pages that follow, is a financial philosophy - a piggy philosophy! It is not legal advice, tax advice, or a promise to make you a millionaire. It's financial inspiration, education and hope for the working class!

After decades of service, studies and work, I'm now pursuing a passion. My mission is simple - "Helping everyday people achieve financial success."

If you're tired of the rat race and crave a life of RICHES, let's go! Together, we can crush the wealth gap and ensure financial success for all, one piggy at a time - I truly hope you'll join me!

                        Sincerely,
                        One Rich Little Pig!

CONTENTS

	Open Letter	
Chapter 1	Piggy Philosophy	1
Chapter 2	Income (A Bounty of Swill)	11
Chapter 3	A Financial House (of Brick)	37
Chapter 4	Budget (Foundation)	47
Chapter 5	Debt (Basement)	63
Chapter 6	Emergency Fund (Pillar)	93
Chapter 7	Retirement (Pillar)	105
Chapter 8	House (Pillar)	129
Chapter 9	Estate Plan (Pillar)	141
Chapter 10	Insurance (Roof)	157
Chapter 11	Hey, Wait A Minute! (College Fund)	175
Chapter 12	Summary (Parting Piggy Thoughts)	187
Appendix A	Action Items	191
Appendix B	Piggy Philosophy	192
Appendix C	Useful & Cool Piggy Links	195
	About the Author	200

CHAPTER 1
PIGGY PHILOSOPHY

Rich. What does it mean to be "rich"? What is a financial house of brick and how do you build one? Being rich means you have freedom. It means you feel safe, secure, and comfortable in your life. You wake up every day, walking on air! Being rich means you live an enjoyable, meaningful life and can retire with dignity. A financial house of brick affords that richness and you're about to learn how to build one - by following a philosophy.

The piggy philosophy is a simple one. It's not filled with tales of how to get rich quick, leverage crafty tax shelters, or compute complex financial formulas. There are no guarantees, no automatic millionaires, and surely, no promises of easy wealth. The philosophy does, however, provide a blueprint for building a sound financial house - one that offers a life of safety, security and comfort. The goal is to provide financial peace of mind, but who knows, you may even get wealthy along the way. This approach is not perfect, foolproof, or "better than" the myriad of others out there, but it does, in fact, *work*! The approach taken is not just a specific micro-focus on money, but rather a *holistic* macro-view of your entire "financial house". In other words, this philosophy is about more than just budgeting, investing, or debt management. You'll discover that building a strong financial house also involves your career path, estate plans, insurance needs, retirement, and more. Therefore, do not make this the only book you read about personal finance because it is not *only* about personal finance. The piggy philosophy goes a bit deeper to describe a way of life that is perhaps different from most. It subscribes to a certain set of *values* and *behaviors* - ones that may not stand out in a mainstream society of razzle-dazzle, glitz and glamour, or materialism. As with any philosophy, people generally follow certain values.

Whether they write them down or not, everyone has values that they live by. This leads to the "pig" in piggy philosophy. Just the image of a storybook pig's life describes the journey of a hard working, humble little guy who, along the way, enjoys the richness of life each and every day. This underdog, working-class citizen not only toils relentlessly towards a goal, but gladly offers a hand-up to others where needed. He also knows how to have plenty of fun along the way! You should not wait to have fun until you retire, complete your degree, or get that promotion. Having fun is a part of every single day. Enjoy the green grass under your feet, the soft sand between your toes, and the warm sunshine on your face. Enjoy being alive, spending time with family, friends and the loved ones you value so dearly. However, do not confuse having fun with spending every penny, buying lots of stuff, or being irresponsible with money. While there are no *right* values in life, these serve as the foundation of piggy philosophy.

Stoicism - the endurance of pain or hardship without a display of feelings and without complaint. 'Rich' does not come easy. Long hours, lots of study, and years of hard work lay ahead - welcome them. Give 100% every day!

Passion - strong and barely controllable emotion. Love for your family and friends will motivate you. *They*...are why you do what you do. You will NOT accept defeat. When the going gets tough, you overcome anything that stands in your way. The engine of success. Live and work like a caged lion who's just been released!

Excellence - the quality of being excellent or extremely good. Your work is not 'good enough' - it is the gold standard. When you're given a job, it's considered DONE. Your income must reflect your work; accept nothing less.

Humility - a modest or low view of one's own importance; humbleness. You did not succeed alone. Substance over flash. You are a smaller part of a larger whole. Embrace success with dignity. Always be grateful.

Generosity - the quality of being kind and generous. Give back. Pay it forward. Offer a hand up. Teach, mentor and coach with empathy. Help others.

The piggy philosophy can be summed up in the motto:

"Work Hard, Play Harder!"

Although not an all-inclusive list, these values provide a strong starting point for living a rich life. They will guide you when times are tough and ground you when times are good. Live them. These *values* should guide your *actions*, particularly those taken to build your financial house. We all know people who are living paycheck to paycheck. You'll hear those same people say "if only I had THAT person's paycheck, I'd be okay." Ironically, THAT person is *also* living paycheck to paycheck and saying "if only I had THAT person's paycheck, I'd be okay." The way to become a rich little piggy is to work hard, study hard, and live within your means. When we were kids, homework always came before going outside to play. Do your homework. Make a temporary sacrifice sooner, for a larger reward later. Being a rich little piggy allows you to focus on what matters. Ponder these questions...

- Do you prefer more time at *work* or with *family*?
- Would you rather go to the *office* or the *beach*?
- If you could afford to, would you retire *sooner* or *later*?
- What's more important, *people* or *stuff*?

Hmm, interesting questions with seemingly obvious answers. Obvious? If so, then why does it seem so many of us spend more waking hours at work than with our families? Why do we choose to retire at age 65 or 70 instead of in our

30s or 40s? Why do we work so darn hard, taking time away from the things (and *people*) we love? *Money* - that's why! We need money to eat, pay rent, afford gas, buy clothes, and much, much more. We need money to live. So, the answer must be money...right? Well if so, why are there so many people with lots of money still slaving away to earn even more? Why do so many celebrities, professional athletes, and social "elites" end up bankrupt, broke, or sitting in jail for tax evasion? If only you could just hit the lotto, right? Why do so many lottery winners end up penniless within a few years? Because focusing on materialism and the tactical micro-aspects of money lead to disaster, regardless of how much you have! Make more, spend more, right? Some of the wealthiest people go broke by focusing exclusively on the *money* piece and neglecting the rest of their financial house (too much debt, inadequate insurance, no budget, no retirement, etc). #FinancialFails!

This brings us back to our piggy philosophy. Rich little piggies not only subscribe to a holistic philosophy, but also follow a macro-level blueprint to build a well-rounded financial house of brick. This ensures you have the proper income, job skills, education, financial foundation, structure, insurance, estate plan, retirement, debt management, and other components necessary to be safe, secure and comfortable. You'll earn more, spend less, and live debt free. But how? How do we get to enjoy the full richness of each and every day? How do we build a solid financial future that allows us to retire with dignity, sooner rather than later? Let's find out how!

As part of the philosophy, there are 6 piggy principles that you must follow. The principles, and a brief explanation of each, are as follows. Do each, in this order.

1. Grow your income
2. Follow a written budget
3. Live debt free
4. Build a 6-month emergency fund
5. Save 10% of income for retirement
6. Pay it forward

1. Grow your income. Following this principle allows you to have more income with which to build your financial house. The strategies listed in Chapter 2 will enable you to live this principle.

2. Follow a written budget. The importance of this principle can not be overstated. A written budget forms the foundation of your entire financial house. Chapter 4 is devoted entirely to creating and following a written budget.

3. Live debt free. This means living a life of cash. Avoiding debt leads to financial freedom. Chapter 5 contains a process for getting out of debt and tips for staying out.

4. Build a 6-month emergency fund. This principle shields you from life's surprises and helps prevent you from falling into debt. Chapter 6 discusses how to build your emergency fund.

5. Save 10% of income for retirement. By saving for retirement, you'll be able to retire with dignity, sooner rather than later. Chapter 7 is dedicated to showing you how to build a nice retirement.

6. Pay it forward. Living the life of a rich little pig is wonderful! However, be sure to lend a hand up to others who may wish to do the same. Living this principle is what makes it all worth it.

As you'll soon discover in Chapter 4, there are many components to building your financial house. Some will apply to you while others may not. For example, you might not ever buy a house and therefore Chapter 8 will not apply to you. You may choose not to have children, in which case Chapter 11 will not apply. However, the aforementioned 6 piggy principles apply to *everyone*. So, regardless of your financial situation in life, be sure to follow these principles. Each will become clearer and explained in further detail as you progress through subsequent chapters.

Following the piggy principles is only part of the equation. Getting a job and managing your finances are the means to the end. You should understand *why* you work. I've always told myself that I work to live, not live to work. That philosophy is simplistic yet powerful. It prioritizes living above working, therefore the less you work, the more you live. The philosophy is to earn more and earn faster, thus allowing you to work less and retire sooner. It's a proven method that simply works. Therefore, you should ask yourself what you're trying to achieve.

Before acting on career or finances, you must *develop a long-term strategy*. Your long-term strategy is the way to your destination - the way to winning. A long-term strategy will help you win the war, but only if you succeed in the smaller battles and medium sized campaigns along the way. These battles and campaigns are your short and mid-term goals - financial stepping stones to success. We'll explore these goals and strategies as they apply to the different components of your financial house. So, with your strategy and goals in mind, it's time to begin your financial journey.

The road to riches is separated into two main stages. The first stage is to *generate income*. It's difficult to get anywhere in life without income. No kidding, you say! This is stating the obvious, yet how many millions of people are no further along today than they were, say, five years ago? Therefore, in the *income stage*, you'll find concrete actions you can take to grow your career and boost your income. However, be advised, our focus in this stage is not so much on career planning. Rather, this first stage places an emphasis on the *need* for income and provides some ways to grow it. Forget about brick, you can't even build a house of *cards* without income. You can find countless books on career counseling; choose one that complements your career path. Once you're earning money, you enter the second stage, which is where we lay out a blueprint on *how to build your financial house (of brick)*. The house you build will determine your financial future. Ok, since our journey consists of two main stages, and times a-wastin', let's move on to our first stage of achieving financial success.

Key Takeaways:

- Piggy Values (live these):
    - Stoicism
    - Passion
    - Excellence
    - Humility
    - Generosity
- Piggy Motto: Work Hard, Play Harder!
- Follow the 6 Piggy Principles (do these, in this order):
    1. Grow your income
    2. Follow a written budget
    3. Live debt free
    4. Build a 6-month emergency fund
    5. Save 10% of income for retirement
    6. Pay it forward
- Develop a Long-term Strategy
    - Have short & mid-term goals to achieve your strategy
- Road to Riches is in Two Stages:
    - Generate Income
    - Build your Financial House

"If you will live like no one else, later you can *live* like no one else." -Dave Ramsey

David W. Robbins

CHAPTER 2
INCOME (A BOUNTY OF SWILL)

Before you can build a financial house of brick, or any house for that matter, you must have INCOME. **A piggy truism is that having too little income is the second biggest reason people have money problems.** (The biggest reason is not having a budget). The more income you have, the easier it is to build a strong house! There are many ways to produce income, but for most of us piggies it starts with a J-O-B. Getting a job is a great way to start growing your income, which happens to be piggy principle #1.

1. **Grow your income**
2. Follow a written budget
3. Live debt free
4. Build a 6-month emergency fund
5. Save 10% of income for retirement
6. Pay it forward

Without getting too far along, let's first acknowledge that having a job is just the beginning - then we'll look at ways to maximize income from our job. Once you land a job, that is not the end. You have only achieved the first step towards your long-term strategy. Growing your income is a never ending endeavor. Your jobs should gradually evolve and mature through added responsibility, advanced skills training, industry certifications, college education, mobility, and ultimately blossom into a full-fledged professional career. You'll see how each of these can advance your earnings potential. Also, since a 'traditional' career is not the only way to make money, we'll also explore self-employment. Lastly, we wrap up with some other possible income streams besides work. Let's see how each of these will help us bring home more bacon!

Get a Job!

To be clear, a **job** is called a "job" for a reason - it requires work. You'll decide what jobs you'll be willing to work in your lifetime and how fulfilling they are, but for our purposes (building a financial house of brick), the goal is to generate *income*! Make no mistake, having fun, working your dream job, and loving what you do are nice qualities to have in a job. However, what's more important is how much you get paid! Pursuing your passion is nice, just as going outside to play is nice. However, you must do your homework first. Doing your homework enables everything else. There's nothing wrong with taking a job that makes you happy or seems 'easy' at the time, but not at the expense of your future. Most jobs that are easy, are easy for a reason

- they pay very little! If you currently have a job, that's a good. Chances are, you have experience under your belt, maybe some college education, and have been to an interview or two (or more). However, if you're about ready to leave the nest, graduate college, or have yet to land your first real job in life, there are ways to get started.

If you've never had a job before, it can be very frustrating trying to figure out *how* to get one and a little unnerving about *what* to expect when you finally *do* get one. **How to get a job** involves matching your skills, education, and experience with the requirements of the job. The less skills, education, and experience you have, the fewer jobs you'll be qualified to fill. At times, this can be down-right depressing and lead a self-defeatist little piggy to pack it in and call it quits. Those are the piggies that live in houses of straw. Since you're building a house of brick and you have the *passion* to succeed, this is where the hard work *starts*! In fact, one of the ways to land a job is to **take one that nobody wants** - maybe it's "too hard", "overly stressful" or has "long hours". Taking a tough job may not be ideal, but it should be viewed as an opportunity to get your foot in the door and build some experience while bringing in *money*. Obviously jobs can be found on **Job Boards** - listings on the Internet, social media sites, bulletin boards, newspaper and magazine classifieds, etc. There are also **internships** and **apprenticeships** available to help secure a well paying job. Internships come in many variations, but generally do not pay a salary - at least not at first. In an internship, you may agree to work unpaid, usually part-time for a company (around your full-time job or college), in exchange for valuable experience, training and/or special hiring preference for new job openings within that company. Similarly, apprenticeships are generally used to gain experience and specialized training, but unlike internships, you <u>will</u> get paid for your work. Apprenticeships may be popular in trades such as electrician, plumber, contractor, etc, and can be very valuable in building your resume. Lastly, don't forget about "who you know." **Networking** is an often overlooked but good way to find a job. Reach out to friends, family, classmates, or neighbors and let them know what type of job you're looking for. They may even know someone who knows someone - leave no rock unturned. There are many factors to consider when selecting a job, but there's one factor that can have a profound impact on your income during your golden years.

Choosing a job that offers certain *retirement benefits* can greatly enhance your income potential when you finally call it quits and retire. There are two big retirement benefits you should look for as part of your employee compensation package: a *retirement account* and a *pension*. When discussing retirement accounts, always seek advice from a certified tax professional. This book intentionally does not reference tax strategies or specifics, such as annual IRA limits, or what items are tax deductible. This is due to the ever changing nature of our complicated tax laws and the differences in each individual's specific circumstances. The intent here is to highlight the power of establishing a retirement account and help you leverage employer benefits to boost your long-term savings. Some employers offer retirement accounts (i.e. 401K) that allow you to build a nest egg for your golden years. Simply offering a retirement account by itself is not the real benefit because, as long as you have earned income, you can open a retirement account on your own. The real benefit is finding an employer that will MATCH funds in your retirement account. How does this work? When you start employment with a company that offers, say, a 401K retirement account, you have the opportunity to save a certain amount of your pay into that account. For example, if you invested $200 per month of your paycheck directly into the account, your company would MATCH your $200 with a certain amount. The matching amount varies by company - some will match only up to a certain percentage, while others will match dollar-for-dollar, up to a set limit. If your company matches dollar-for-dollar, they would match your $200 with an additional $200, giving you a total monthly contribution of $400 into your retirement account (only $200 of which came out of your own paycheck)...pretty sweet! The challenge is finding an employer that provides that type of match. Even if you can get a 50% match, that's still a very nice benefit (you'd invest $200 and they'd invest $100). Essentially, employer matches can be viewed as instant return-on-investment. If you receive a 50% company match, that's basically saying you're earning 50% interest on every dollar you invest into your retirement account - from the minute you put it there! There are annual limits to how much you're allowed to contribute to retirement accounts, which often change, so again, be sure to consult a certified tax professional before investing. We'll talk more about retirement accounts in Chapter 7, but it bears mentioning here because choosing a job that offers one can be a very good benefit. A retirement account is not the only retirement benefit you should look for.

Going the way of the dinosaur, one retirement benefit that can contribute significantly to your golden years is a *pension*. Decades ago, it was the 'norm' that you'd go work at the local factory or some big 'blue chip' company (GE, IBM, Ford, etc) for 30 years and when you retired, you'd get a gold watch and a monthly pension for the rest of your life. Those days are all but gone! If you do find a private company that still pays a pension, please be sure to post it all over social media so the rest of the world knows about it. Today, with few exceptions, building a sound retirement is in YOUR hands. {If you're thinking Social Security, save that thought for Chapter 7.} So, if you're looking for a job that offers a pension, you'll increase your chances by looking to the public sector. Although our elected officials are always looking for ways to cut....ahem...I mean streamline benefits, you can still find public sector jobs that offer a pension. There are federal, state, county, and city agencies that offer pensions, provided you meet the eligibility criteria. As with most things, job benefits come with pros and cons; public sector jobs that offer pensions will typically pay lower wages than an equivalent private sector job that does not offer a pension. By and large, you have a choice of *higher* salary with *fewer* retirement benefits, or a *lower* salary with *more* retirement benefits. This is not stamped in stone or some new scientific law by any means - it's simply a general rule of thumb. Just as you would shop around when buying an expensive item, such as a new car, you should also do so when looking for a job. Federal jobs that offer pensions will vary slightly by which retirement system you're enrolled in. If you're interested in a state, county, or city job, be sure to check how each funds its pension system and understand all of the other benefits it offers before considering employment. Under the right conditions, accepting a lower salary for a healthy pension can pay off in the long run. So, how about having your cake and eating it too?

If you want BOTH a *pension* and a *retirement account*, continue your job search in the public sector. For example, most federal employees are eligible to invest in the Thrift Savings Plan (a retirement account), *and* are also eligible to receive a pension, after accumulating so many years of service. Some federal agencies will also match your retirement contributions, up to a certain percentage. So, depending on the agency you're interested in working for, some will offer not only a pension, but the opportunity to invest in a retirement account also (and potentially a match)! In fact, many people overlook a fantastic opportunity to work for an organization that offers many of these benefits - the military. Joining a branch of the military can be a rich and rewarding experience. You will receive a steady income, education benefits, medical and dental benefits, and if you serve long enough, earn a retirement pension. In terms of a retirement account, serving in the military also allows you to contribute to the Thrift Savings Plan. Additionally, the military will teach you valuable leadership and technical skills that can be used when you transition to civilian life. Again, whether it's the private sector or the public sector, it's important to do your research before deciding on a job. There are resources included in Appendix

C that may be helpful in your search.

One factor to consider when trying to decide if you want a job that offers a pension is *vesting*. The term *vesting* can have various meanings, but here it means having completed the requirements in order to receive a pension with a given company/agency (provided they offer one). Typically, you must be employed for a certain amount of *time* with the company/agency before you're eligible to receive a pension. For example, you may have to work for 5 years with a federal agency to collect a minimal pension when you reach a certain age (i.e. 62). The longer you work with the agency, the larger your pension will be. A formula is normally applied to determine how much your annual/monthly pension will be, depending on certain factors. Some variable factors that can affect your pension are: length of time with agency, highest salary earned while employed with agency, date of hire (which pension program you're enrolled in), breaks in employment, unpaid absences, and more. Some agencies will calculate your pension based upon the average of your highest 3 years of earnings, while others may calculate it based upon the average 5 years of earnings and so on. Some pension requirements can be complex and vesting requirements may vary over time - therefore no specifics are listed here in this section. However, there are links/resources pertaining to pensions in Appendix C. Why is it important to consider vesting?

Imagine you've been employed with an agency for 4 years and they offer vesting after at least 5 years of employment. This means if you work for them at least 5 years, you're eligible for a minimal pension at age 62. Now imagine you discover (or are offered) a job at a separate company that offers a 20% increase in salary! The catch is, they don't offer a pension and you're not vested in your current job for at least 1 more year - ouch! What do you do? What if the new job offered a 25% salary increase, or 30%? What are you willing to give up in exchange for "something better"? These are critical career choices that, ideally, should be thought out in some fashion beforehand. Obviously, you don't have a crystal ball and can't possibly map out your entire life's career before it even starts. However, you should be prepared to do your homework and at least have a basic plan. Remember, you must develop short and mid-term goals, with an overall long-term strategy in mind. Don't just wing it. Pigs can't fly - yet. When applying for a job that offers a pension, ask yourself if you're prepared to work there for at least the minimum number of years required to be vested. If something better comes along after that point, at least you will not lose everything you've worked for up until then. On the other hand, are you more comfortable taking jobs with much higher salaries, in lieu of the security of a pension? Questions, questions. There are no "correct" answers to these questions, but it is correct for you to consider these scenarios and do your research as early as possible. You are also correct to periodically re-assess your career situation every few years or so, to ensure you're on the right path (long-term strategy).

When applying for any job, it's a good idea to talk to the Human Resources department before you start, or at least within a few weeks of starting your new job. Most companies will educate new hires on their benefits package automatically as part of their company/agency training policy, but if not, be sure to ask - it's YOUR career! So, retirement accounts and pensions are a major employment consideration, but they are not the only ones.

When growing your career, you must also consider insurance against life's surprises. For example, a major factor contributing to debt and bankruptcy today is medical bills. If you can find a job that offers a good healthcare plan, it can help you reduce expenses and provide better coverage for not *if*, but *when* you need it. In addition to healthcare insurance, you must consider what happens if you're unable to work. Do you have disability insurance? If not, you may suffer a huge financial storm should you be unable to work. Automobile accidents happen all the time. Slips, falls, injuries, illness, and more can derail the best laid financial plan if you do not have disability insurance. We'll talk more on this topic in Chapter 10, but it also applies right here, right now as you consider your plan for employment. These are all factors to think about as you start, and continue, your career. Once you land a job that offers the best benefits possible, don't stop there!

Responsible...Who, Me?!

The first few jobs you work should be thought of as stepping stones - as a chance to build experience, and **add responsibilities** to your resume. So, how do you add responsibility to your resume? By going above and beyond - by doing *more* than the bare minimum. How often have you heard "that's not my job", or "it's not in my duty description"? The little piggies working those jobs normally go home at the end of the day to a house of straw. They're not very motivated, and as a consequence, don't normally move up the proverbial corporate ladder. Ironically, those are the people that are also quick to complain about management not doing this or not doing that, but when given the opportunity to become management, they're all talk. Don't fall into the trap of laziness and just getting by. Remember, *excellence* defines your work. Ask your supervisor how you can learn different aspects of the job. Talk to your co-workers who have been there longer than you have and learn *why* something is done the way it is and how it can be done *better* (faster, cheaper, safer, etc). If you work the cash register, try to learn warehousing and operations also. If you're a waiter or waitress, offer to help with food preparation or supply management when times are slow. Computer programmers may want to shadow the project manager for a few days in order to learn the 'big picture' of *why* they're coding the software applications in a certain manner.

It's often said that humility is an admirable trait, but don't let it morph into bashfulness when it comes to your job. Let your boss know what you're doing! Tell your supervisor you want to succeed and ask him or her how you can do so. If they offer little help, or resist your efforts, it's time to look for a new job. Either find new work, or stay there whining for the next few years. Your career is in *your* hands - don't be short-changed by a lackadaisical boss. All the while, do not burn bridges. You want to maintain a good working relationship with your supervisor and co-workers. These folks will most likely be your source of references for future job applications. So, not only should you add as much responsibility to your resume as possible, but there are even more things you can do to further your career.

"Skills Training, Advance! Hut, two, three four..."

Obtaining **advanced skills training** in your field is a fantastic way to increase your value as an employee. Yes, more money! Certain professions require use of specialized equipment. You must have advanced skills in order to operate that specialized equipment, and will therefore be more marketable. Advanced skills can be obtained by attending trade schools, technical schools, classroom training, self-study courses and completing online classes. Heavy equipment operators require a license for each class of vehicle they operate (forklift, bulldozer, tractor trailer, etc). The more licenses to operate they have, the more money they'll make. Network administrators can obtain advanced training on the latest in-demand software applications, again, increasing the salary they can demand. It's important to note that advanced skills training is normally on-going and never-ending. In today's fast-paced world, things rarely stay the same for long and employees must continuously seek out new training opportunities for the next 'latest and greatest' thing (tool, technology, application, equipment, device, process, etc). Fortunately, some employers will provide advanced skills training to you at their own expense. In fact, you may consider applying for certain jobs for this very reason - because they'll pay for training! If they don't come right out and offer it, sometimes it helps to *ask* your employer to pay for your training. You have nothing to lose, right? If you decide to do this, be sure to show your supervisor how obtaining the training will help you perform your job better, thereby helping the company's bottom line (profitability, increased sales, faster customer service, etc). In the event your company does not provide training, you may consider paying for it yourself. When doing so, give careful consideration to your return on investment. Paying for a class that will not increase your chances of earning more money within the next year is probably a waste of money. However, if you pay for a class that will increase your salary by at least the cost of the class within a year, it may be worth it. Do not borrow money for advanced skills training. If you can't pay cash, don't take the class. If money is tight, a self-study course may be more appropriate than the class. Sometimes you can spend $50 on a book and learn almost as much through self-study as you can through a classroom course that costs a few thousand dollars. It may just take a little longer. Given enough specialized training, you will want to consider upping your game.

I'm Certifiably Certifiable!

A notch above specialized training in your career is obtaining **industry certifications** (also known as professional certifications). Some industries offer more certifications than others, but by and large, they all serve relatively the same purpose - to "certify" you as possessing certain baseline knowledge and/or skills and expertise within your profession or industry. This might include project management, computer security, electrician, physical therapy, and much more. Obtaining certifications can be difficult and requirements vary from one profession or industry to the next. Be sure to conduct research to ensure you pursue the certification that's right for you. Many industries have professional association websites that can refer you to legitimate certification authorities and help guide you through the process. Some certifying authorities will demand documented proof of your work history to verify that you have performed the specific type of work required for certification (i.e. electrical, programming, etc). This documented proof normally requires you to list your related job experience and obtain signatures of previous employers/supervisors to verify that you have, in fact, performed that type of work.

Most certifications require you to take a test and achieve a minimum passing score. No need to worry though, because you can usually find various study guides online to help you prepare for the test. Furthermore, a few certifications will have to be maintained by completing so many annual hours, or credits, of continuing education related to the specialized profession. Some certifications refer to them as Professional Development Units (PDU), whereas others may call them Continuing Professional Education (CPE), and so on. No matter the terminology, the requirement is to ensure a certified member stays current in the discipline they're certified in by means of on-going education. You typically complete your PDUs or CPEs over a given time period by reading specific material, taking quizzes, short courses, self-study, or online training in your industry or field of certification. Once complete, you upload completion of your work to their website for credit. Each certification has its own time period requirements (i.e. 30 PDUs per year, 60 CPEs every 3 years, etc). It may seem rigorous at first, but you'll soon realize the value it adds. After all, wouldn't you want to ensure your dentist remained current on the latest dental procedures? Or your electrician to stay current on new building codes and wiring safety standards? Industry certifications let your employer and prospective employers know that you are a true professional, dedicated to your trade. As such, you can generally demand a much higher salary when you obtain professional certifications. Some are so important to their field, they mean more than a college degree! Speaking of college degrees - where are you at with yours?

Look Ma, I'm College Edumucated.

Whether you landed your first job straight out of high school or after you complete a **college degree**, there's always room for more college education. That is, if you wish to grow your income. If you already possess a bachelor's degree, this may mean going for a masters degree, then maybe on to a doctorate. *Can* you do well without a degree? *Can* you be the rare entrepreneur who drops out of school and becomes rich? Yes. Yes, you can. Just like you can make it in show business or professional sports - yes, you can. However, in most people's reality and most certainly in today's world, a college education will *help* you far more than it will *hurt* you. The conversation around college can be a funny one. From sky-rocketing tuition costs and crushing student loan debt, to whether an industry certification or a college degree is more valuable, tempers can flare. Calm down and take a deep breath. Yes, some would argue that a college degree is no longer necessary or too 'old school' to be successful in the new high-technology, social media, dot-com, entrepreneurial landscape. Those are the same little piggies that would argue a house of straw will do just fine. Wrong! If you want a financial house of straw, stop reading now and give this book to another little piggy who prefers a financial house of brick! Getting a college degree should be the backbone of your career. If you're doing just fine right now without a degree, get one - you'll do even better! Surround your degree with work experience, advanced skills training, and industry certifications, but *get* a college degree. There are two main considerations when choosing a degree: *field of study* and *cost*.

Choose your *field of study* based upon a number of factors, not just what interests you. Basket weaving may be interesting (to some), but it will not pay the bills! Be realistic. Chances are good that you've held *some* kind of job before starting college and can use that work experience as a starting point for school. If you're coming straight out of high school, it may have been a summer job, internship, or part-time nights/weekend job, doing something you enjoy. In this case, it may not be as important if your field of study is different from the work you performed in those jobs. However, suppose you've been working in a certain field for the last 8-10 years (for example, network administration), and decide to start a degree plan. Choosing a degree in something unrelated to network administration (i.e. chemistry, biology, or philosophy) is "costing" you those 8-10 years of experience in network administration. The intent here is not to pick on one field of study or the other, but to illustrate the fact that if you already have 8-10 years of experience doing something, it's far more advantageous to get a degree that complements that work. That's not to say changing careers or fields of study can't, or shouldn't be done. Many people change careers to pursue something they love. However, changing your field of study in mid-career should be carefully thought out before doing so because it comes at a cost. Once you've invested so many years into a profession, it becomes far more beneficial in terms of salary to match your college degree with your work. Likewise, if you attend college right out of high school and get a degree in computer science, you wouldn't want to start applying for pharmacist jobs. That just wouldn't make sense. Nothing against pharmacists, but that means you just completely wasted your time and money earning a computer science degree. Talking with college counselors and job placement specialists can help you decide on a realistic and lucrative degree plan. Remember, a college degree is likely a mid-term goal. You want a degree that is in high demand and will remain so for a long time. Today, there are so many colleges, universities and degree plans to choose from, that it's fairly easy to find a degree plan that is both interesting and will make you more marketable. However, field of study is not your only consideration when selecting a degree.

Deciding on a college degree plan also involves choosing a school to attend. The choice can range from fairly affordable to astronomically expensive - consider *cost* carefully! Picking the wrong school can leave you saddled with a mountain of crushing student loans. However, the goods news is that there are many schools to choose from, many of which are quite affordable. There may be exceptions but generally speaking, all other things being equal, public schools are more affordable than private ones. Whether you attend a private or public school makes no matter; be sure you can afford it!

Given that you meet the application criteria and once you're accepted to the school of your choice, it's now time to focus like a laser on paying tuition (plus any other fees; room/board, books, etc). It's critical to pay as much tuition as possible as you go. Do not let your tuition fees accumulate. This is where research can help immensely. Some sources and ideas for financial assistance are listed below. There are more resources and links in Appendix C. Also be sure to talk to the admissions office at your school (or prospective school) to see what help is available. If you're already employed when you make the decision to attend college, start tightening your budget immediately. More on budgeting in Chapter 4. You'll want to budget enough money each month to pay as much tuition as possible, if not, all of it. Depending on your salary and the cost of tuition, this may not be realistic, but NOW is the moment to plan that out - don't wait until you're under a huge debt load! There is no single "cookie cutter" approach for paying tuition. Depending where you are in your stage of career/life, there are numerous ways to afford a valuable and in-demand college degree without a mountain of student loans at graduation. Some options for minimizing student debt are as follows:

- Scholarships.
- Grants.
- Financial aid from family (or the school itself).
- Select a college with affordable tuition rates.
- Military service offers education benefits, tuition assistance, GI Bill, etc.
- Pay-as-you-go; work overtime, extra job, etc.
- Company benefits may pay full, or partial tuition.
- Borrow <u>least</u> amount possible.

When factoring college costs, also be sure to research average starting salaries for employees with the degree you plan on getting. Again, there is not a single cookie-cutter formula to apply here. For example, if you have a full scholarship for any state university of your choosing, then tuition really doesn't matter, it's not coming out of your pocket. You may get partial help from grants or parents that cover half of tuition costs, or somewhere in between. It's pretty hard *not* to get *any* financial help from *somewhere*, but in a worst-case scenario, you then must weigh the cost of tuition against your projected salary. Keep it reasonable and pay as much as you can, as you go. You want the smallest student loan debts possible upon graduation, if any at all. If you project a total student loan debt that's more than your projected starting annual salary in that particular field, stop! Time out. This is time to re-examine your college costs and financial aid options. Some may argue otherwise, but you do not want total student loan debt higher than your starting annual salary. At that point, there is little return on investment and it will take far too long to dig out of debt. If required, dig deeper for financial assistance - your challenge is to find the options that are out there! Working overtime and/or an extra job for a year or so is a good way to stockpile cash to pay for tuition. Be aggressive. Remember, working a side job or putting in a bunch of overtime is *temporary* and will save you *years* of paying off loans and interest! Should you fall into the student loan quicksand, it can mean decades of debt, stress, and headache. In a nutshell, the goal is to get a college degree, with no student loan debt, and leverage each higher-level degree for a higher salary. Yes, more money! Whether it's before *or* after getting your degree, don't limit your job search to only one specific location.

A Rolling Stone...

In addition to increased training and education, an often overlooked but proven way to increase your salary is to remain *mobile*. Being mobile simply means that you're willing to relocate (get up and move) for a better paying job! This power can not be overstated. Think about it, sitting and waiting for a job to become available within a few miles of where you live can result in a lot of waiting. A *good* job may actually *never* become available. Beggars can't be choosers, so if you want a job near you, be prepared to accept whatever is offered. However, the wider you open your job search, the more jobs you have to choose from. Consider opening your job search to city, state, nation, or even world-wide. While it's true there may be associated moving costs, the benefits will far outweigh those costs. How do you know that for sure? Simple, because you don't move unless it's worth it. In other words, if it will cost you 'X' amount of dollars to move, ensure you negotiate a salary that will be worth it before agreeing to move. You might seek a raise in salary equal to *at least* triple your moving costs. For example, you currently make $50,000/year and the move will cost $4,000. If you triple the moving costs of $4,000, you want a new job that offers at least $12,000 more than your current job. Therefore, you don't move for less than a new salary of *at least* $62,000. Besides, some employers will actually pay your moving expenses. It happens a lot more than you'd think, so don't be afraid to ask. In addition to a higher salary, you can also bank some serious money.

Another proven mobility tactic is to live on the cheap in an area with a high cost of living (hint, high pay). The goal is to move to where the money is, live below your means and save the bulk of your pay. You can live in a down-sized apartment, a no-frills rental unit, or even a small 1-bedroom loft. Taking on a roommate or two is another good way to minimize living expenses. If you live in a city with good public transportation, you may not even need a car. This would save you even more money. In addition to saving serious money you can also leverage your higher salary.

When you have a high salary, you can use it to obtain an even higher one. Many employers and job recruiters use your current salary as a starting point for salary negotiations. The idea is to use each salary as a stepping stone to the next.

Moving every year or two can double your pay in no time. In a few moves, you can go from $45,000 to $60,000 to $75,000 or more, all the while gaining new skills and a beefed up resume. Before you know it, six figures are next and then you live anywhere you want. That's how it's done! Growing your career through mobility can be a rewarding experience, but if and when you ever become tired of 'traditional' jobs, there are other endeavors to pursue.

My Own Boss!

When most people think of a job, they picture a daily commute to the office, a 9-to-5 schedule, reporting to the boss, staff meetings, cubicles, weekly paydays, and other such visions of work. However, don't be afraid to consider self-employment or entrepreneurial endeavors (aka working for yourself). Generally speaking, there's more risk with owning your own business and working for yourself, but the potential reward is also greater. The rich little piggy path to building a financial house of brick *starts* with a traditional job, but can eventually branch out to self-employment or starting your own business. Horror stories abound of individuals with solid, stable, decent paying jobs, venturing out to start their own business and ending up in bankruptcy. This is because they were unprepared. This chapter, or even this book, is not about entrepreneurship. We will not cover self-employment "how-to's", tax strategies, business plans, advertising pitfalls, roadmaps to success, or anything specific to being an entrepreneur. It's mentioned here for two reasons. First, self-employment can be a lucrative source of income if executed *properly* thus, included in the

INCOME chapter. Secondly, when it comes to building your financial house of brick, self-employment can be a disaster if executed *improperly*. Generally speaking, it's difficult to suffer huge income losses and debt from a traditional, 9-to-5, employer-based job. Here, we're talking about debt from the job itself; traditional jobs do not require you to invest your personal funds as with your own business. However, it's much easier to get caught in a financial disaster when you're in business for yourself. Just a few landmines include insufficient liability insurance, malpractice, lawsuits, incorrect tax filings, compliance with state and local laws, employee labor laws, equipment costs, and much more. If you're sincerely interested in working for yourself, there are some resources listed in Appendix C that may be of assistance. You can also find countless books on self-employment and entrepreneurship. Again, self employment can be quite a rewarding and lucrative endeavor, but the rich little piggy path starts with a good old fashioned *job*! Once you're financially stable, you may want to explore this avenue. Besides having a great job or working for yourself, there are other sources of income that you may encounter during your lifetime.

$ - Bank Error in Your Favor - $

Other sources of income can include an inheritance, sale of property, investments, alimony, child support, gifts, annuity from a lawsuit, or even a lottery jackpot (keep dreaming!). Any source of income, planned or unplanned, can be used to help build your financial house. Although this type of income probably occurs less often than pay from our job, it must still be counted in our overall income stream. Some folks might be tempted to treat unplanned income as "found money" and blow it all. As with any sudden windfall, there are some factors to consider before you act. How many stories have you heard of lotto winners ending up bankrupt?! Somebody wins "$1 Million", and they start spending like crazy! They drive to the lottery office in a brand new Mercedes. By the time they cash the ticket, complete the paperwork, and possibly elect a lump sum payment, the winnings are now down to $600,000. Next, Uncle Sam wants his cut, so now the winnings are down to about $350,000. So much for being a millionaire. Without proper planning and accounting for tax consequences, a blessing can quickly turn into a nightmare. Depending on how quickly and how much that lotto winner spent, they could be on the hook for *more* than they won! Now, it's not too likely that any of us will win the lotto jackpot, but people do come into unexpected money more often than you'd think, and of varying amounts. Every tax season, people file their tax returns and many will spend the refund before it even hits their bank account. Whether you get an inheritance or maybe you sell some stock, be sure to project any tax consequences before spending the money. When in doubt, consult a certified tax professional. So, any income you receive in addition to your weekly paycheck should be reviewed for tax consequences and then added to your overall income stream. Your total income stream will be used to build and maintain your financial house. This brings us to the second stage of achieving financial success - how to build a financial house. Not just any financial house, but a strong, solid one of brick!

KEY TAKEAWAYS
- Grow your income (always)!
- Get a Job
    - Consider a job with retirement benefits;
        Pensions and retirement accounts can be valuable!
    - Seek Healthcare Benefits;
        This can save you hundreds of dollars monthly.
- Grow Your Career
    - Added Responsibility;
        Work like a beast & always learn.
    - Advanced Skills Training;
        Sharpen your skills to a razor's edge.
    - Industry Certifications;
        Show you're a committed professional.
    - College Degree;
        Get one. Your goal is to graduate debt free!
    - Mobility;
        Be willing to move to where the money is.
- Self-Employment
- Other Income
    - Child Support
    - Alimony
    - Rental Property
    - Investments

"The difference between ordinary and extraordinary is that little extra." -Jimmy Johnson

CHAPTER 3
A FINANCIAL HOUSE (OF BRICK)

As with many endeavors in life, achieving financial success is a building process. At some point in time, a world-class Olympian swimmer started by first learning how to swim. A famous painter most certainly started by first doodling with a box of crayons. Building your financial house is no different. So, as with any building process, regardless of where you are with your finances, it's hard to go wrong if you follow a blueprint. Once you understand the blueprint, you'll be able to assess where you are financially and what steps are necessary in order to move forward. Obviously not everyone is currently at the same financial stage in life. For example, you may be debt free, but don't yet have an emergency fund. You may be saving for retirement, but are still in debt. Regardless of your status, look to the blueprint for a guide on how to build your financial house. Follow it. However, before getting to the blueprint, there are two important factors to keep in mind.

The first factor to keep in mind when following your blueprint is one of financial *focus*. It's true that too many people never achieve financial success because they simply give up trying. They give up trying because they feel it's impossible and they feel it's impossible because they're trying to do too much at once! One major area where people lose financial focus is paying off debt.

You'll never pay off that car loan while taking vacations, buying gifts, and saving for your kid's college fund. You'll never get rid of your credit cards if your living expenses are out of control, your budget is not prioritized, and you're simultaneously trying to save for retirement. Your efforts must be *focused* in order to be effective. Although the piggy blueprint is not a precise step-by-step, sequential process, you'll soon discover that it *does* provide a pay prioritization that should be followed if you wish to be successful. By focusing your spending where it counts, you'll be far more effective. Paying off certain things before others will help your chances of moving to the next financial phase in life. For example, as you'll see, it's necessary to first build your emergency fund before saving for retirement. While you're building your emergency fund, you will not be spending any other money except for bare essential living expenses. At times, you'll be tempted to break away from the process. You'll try to accomplish more than one financial goal at a time. It will seem to difficult to throw every dollar you make towards your debt, but don't give up! Temporary sacrifices will be necessary for a life time of financial freedom. This is true not only in paying off debt, but also in maximizing your income.

Too many folks spend more money than they make each month. It's one thing to pay off debt and slash expenses, but you must always grow your income. At times, you'll be required to focus your work efforts like a laser! Remember your piggy values. When times are tough, *stoicism* and *passion* are your thunder and lightning. Use them to focus on each financial goal, bringing you one step closer to the finish line. If you've hit hard financial times, you must temporarily get hog-wild serious about earning more money. When the chips are down, you are a lion that has just been set free. Live and work like it. If 40 hours per week are not bringing in enough income to meet your goal, you must work 50, 60, or more - get it done! Focusing on maximizing your income for a 6-month period can provide a serious boost to your financial health. The more you earn, the faster you pay off debt. The sooner you pay off debt, the earlier you can retire. Ensure your values drive your career, particularly stoicism and passion. Remember, they are not merely words. As you achieve financial focus, you must also live a certain lifestyle.

The second factor to remember while building your financial house is to live a life of *cash*. I'd argue this is even more difficult than focusing your efforts. It's tough, but you can do it. You must. Living a life of cash does not mean you walk around with a bag full of dollar bills, literally paying cash for everything. Rather, it involves paying for things as you go. That means saving up the money for a product or service and paying cash when you purchase it. The piggy philosophy recognizes this concept as delayed gratification. Just like doing our chores before playing, or eating dinner before having dessert, we even teach our children the benefits of delayed gratification. There are, however, adults who have not yet learned the benefits of delayed gratification. Sadly, those adults have also learned the consequences of their actions - less gratification in life. Living a life of cash will allow you the gratification and freedom you never thought possible. When you buy something, you'll actually own it, instead of owing on it. But why not a life of credit?

Living a life of cash means that you will **not** live a life of credit. Sadly, our society is one of credit and borrowing. Our government owes nearly $18 Trillion dollars, cumulative student loan debt is about $1 Trillion more, and people are still underwater in their homes. If that isn't enough, Edmunds.com, a popular online resource for automotive information recently reported that 55 percent of car loans in 2012 were for a term of more than 5 years. Also, Experian Automotive, an automotive division of the popular credit bureau reports that nearly a quarter of new loans in early 2014 were for terms between 73 and 84 months. That's a 7 year car loan! Yes, the housing bubble has burst, but we've replaced it with student loan and car bubbles. A national brand furniture store recently ran an advertisement offering to finance your furniture for 8 years. Wow, really?! Maybe we'll have a furniture bubble soon too. Borrowing our life away has led us to where we are today, as a nation. This is not new, you already know this. So, what to do about it?

Living on credit is obviously not working, so you must do something different. Live like a rich little piggy while others live on credit. Don't follow the herd - they inevitably go over the cliff. Do you *own* a nice car, or *owe* on a nice car? Do you *own* nice things, or *owe* on nice things that you charged to your credit cards? You want to *own*, not *owe* - there's a big difference. But the Joneses have it and by gosh, I'm going to have it too. News flash - the Joneses are broke too! Some people wander down the credit path in life because they're brainwashed that everything must go on credit. We are constantly bombarded with offers of easy payments, no money down, 0% interest, and free layaway! Unfortunately, an entire industry has evolved because of credit. Yes, it's true that your credit history and credit score are being used more and more often today. Insurance companies are using it to determine your premiums, lenders are using it to calculate your interest rates, and more employers are even using it for hiring decisions. However, you must understand the piggy philosophy is crystal clear when it comes to debt. Your goal is to live debt free. If you follow the principles, your credit score will matter less and less as time goes on. Do not go into debt just because you believe it will help your credit score. In fact, let's look at credit score basics.

A lot of people will often ask "what's my credit score"? Well, which one are they referring to? There are hundreds of scoring models used in the industry and they vary by reporting bureau, lender, model type, and more. The one arguably most well known is the FICO score. FICO (Fair Isaac and Company) developed a model that is used by most lenders to determine your credit worthiness and risk, based upon a number of factors. There are three main credit bureaus that report FICO scores: Experian, Equifax, and TransUnion. Oddly enough, their scores will usually vary due to how much credit history is in your file. For example, you may have a higher score from Experian than from Equifax, or vice versa because one of them does not have a full credit history on you. Not to be outdone, the three main credit bureaus have also developed their own scoring model to compete with the FICO model. Their proprietary model is called the Vantage Score. Like FICO, the Vantage scoring model has its own criteria used to calculate your credit worthiness. Regardless of the scoring model, do not borrow money in the hopes of boosting your credit score.

This book will not discuss scoring models or the criteria used, since borrowing money to improve your credit score is not the way to a sound financial future. If you're interested in learning more about what factors affect your credit score and the three main bureaus, there are entire books available on the topic. You can also obtain a free copy of your credit report from the Annual Credit Report site. Also, Credit Karma advertises free credit scores and has become fairly popular. Both sites are listed in Appendix C. However, keep in mind that if you follow all of the piggy principles, your credit score will take care of itself. So, instead of obsessing over your credit score, ask yourself what a financial house of brick can do.

If a hurricane was coming, would you prefer to live in a house of straw or a house of brick? Me, I'd want to live in a house of brick! Now, what if you were suddenly in a bad car accident and unable to work for an extended period of time? Or you lost your job next week? What if your house got flooded? Would you prefer a financial house of *straw*, or a financial house of *brick*? Once again, I'd choose the **FINANCIAL HOUSE OF BRICK**! Building one of *straw* leaves you susceptible to stress, headaches, unpaid bills, smothering debt, bankruptcy, evictions, foreclosure, repossessions, and more. Well, if you would too - if you'd choose to live in a rock-solid financial house of *brick*, rather than a pathetic, flimsy financial house of *straw*, it's time to get serious. I don't mean kinda serious, sorta serious, or even kinda-sorta serious. I'm talking about full-speed ahead, no excuses, time to get HOG WILD, kick-@$$...serious! Enough running in the hamster wheel. It's time to get your bricks together, build your financial house and start living like a rich little pig. Your boss isn't going to build it for you. Neither will your neighbors, your parents, or the federal government. If you want a rock-solid financial house, YOU must build it...so let's get started TODAY!

By the way, if anyone ever asks "when should I start building my financial house?" The answer is always "now". It may not be easy and there are no simple pre-canned steps to follow. As in life, there are many "what ifs" when building a financial house and sometimes the answer to solving a problem is "it depends". To help minimize those "what ifs" and to reduce the level of uncertainty in building your financial house, you must start with a blueprint.

The blueprint to your financial house will provide a

roadmap for building your finances. It contains key components such as a strong *foundation* (budget) and 4 solid *pillars* (emergency fund, retirement, house, estate plan) that support a *roof* (insurance) to shield you from the financial storms of life. The *basement* (debt) is meant to be clean, dry, finished living space. However, if you don't manage your finances properly, your debt will quickly become a rising cesspool of sewage, threatening to flood your entire house. So, it's important to understand each of the key components to your financial house, what they are, and how to build them. As you'll soon discover, laying a solid *foundation* is the first place to start.

Key Takeaways:
- Build a financial house of *brick* over one of *straw*.
- *Focus* your financial efforts to achieve your goals.
- Live a life of *cash* over one of *credit*.
- Maintain good credit, but don't borrow to achieve it.
- Follow a financial blueprint.
    - Budget (foundation)
    - Debt (basement)
    - Emergency Fund (pillar)
    - Retirement (pillar)
    - House (pillar)
    - Estate Plan (pillar)
    - Insurance (roof)

"Today I will do what others won't, so tomorrow I can do what others can't." -Jerry Rice

David W. Robbins

CHAPTER 4
BUDGET (FOUNDATION)

The foundation of any financial house is a ***budget***. A budget? What the heck is a budget?! Some people believe a budget is just a list of their monthly bills. Others will say a budget is living on peanut butter sandwiches. To some people, budget is a dirty word! The Merriam-Webster online dictionary defines 'budget' as "an amount of money available for spending that is based on a plan for how it will be spent." Pretty simple, right? It's even simpler if you break it down into two parts...

The first part, "an amount of money available for spending" is your INCOME (remember, job). Most people have this.

The second part, "a plan for how it will be spent" is where the magic happens. It involves purposefully spending every dollar of income. Most people don't have this.

So, for our purposes (building a bad-@$$ financial brick house), **a budget is a written plan on how to spend your income**. We modified the dictionary version just a bit to fit our needs. It's a little shorter and we've added that the plan is to be <u>written</u>. You will assign <u>each dollar</u> of income that you earn to (fill-in-the-blank); utility bills, food, clothing, savings, retirement, etc. This will be done in writing! No matter how you slice and dice the definition, it bears repeating that your *budget* will be the foundation of your financial brick house! **A piggy truism is that failing to follow a written budget is the number one reason people have money problems.** It's not by coincidence that following a written budget is piggy principle #2, right after growing your income.

1. Grow your income
2. **Follow a written budget**
3. Live debt free
4. Build a 6-month emergency fund
5. Save 10% of income for retirement
6. Pay it forward

Ok, so now that you know *what* a budget is, you need to learn *how* to build one. Building a budget, in its simplest form, is writing down how you're going to spend every dollar of your income. Don't get hung up on how fancy it should be, what software program to use, or any specific format. Keep it simple. Heck, you can write a budget on the back of a napkin! However, using a spreadsheet of some kind makes it very easy. There are many ways to track income and expenses on your budget spreadsheet, but did I mention I like to keep things simple?

In order to keep things simple, we'll use Phil T. Pig as an example. Phil's biography and his budget worksheet are provided below. As we progress through each chapter, building a new component of our financial house, we'll refer back to Phil. We'll track changes in his **biography**, his **financial status**, and his **budget**. It goes without saying, but I'll say it anyway, please realize this is by no means the ONLY way to create a budget. Do not force your budget to look like this one, but rather tailor it to suit your own situation. This is a SAMPLE for illustration purposes only. Don't get hung up on his salary or his expenses, they're simply examples. Phil's sample budget will be referenced in subsequent chapters of the book as well.

You can see Phil's biography below. It contains some key information about his life. We'll track his progress as we continue through the book.

Biography:

Name:	Phil T. Pig
Age:	25
Marital Status:	Single
Children:	None
Profession:	Electrician
Salary:	$40,320 (take-home)
Retirement Age:	65
Retirement Dream:	Fly Fish & Travel all 50 States
Home Status:	Renting

Next, you can see Phil's key financial status. We'll track his progress throughout each chapter.

Financial Status:

Financial Component	Status
Income	**Started; Growing**
Budget	**Complete**
Debt	Chapter 5
Emergency Fund	Chapter 6
Retirement	Chapter 7
House	Chapter 8
Estate Plan	Chapter 9
Insurance	Chapter 10
College Fund	Chapter 11

Notice the only items visible in Phil's financial status is his Income and his Budget (items in **bold**). The other seven items are grayed out for now; we'll cover those in each respective chapter.

Lastly, is Phil's budget worksheet. As noted, this is just a sample budget. His income is listed at the top, followed by his monthly expenses. His monthly expenses are divided into two main categories; discretionary and essential living expenses. At the bottom of his budget, you'll find total expenses and "excess", meaning what he has left over at the end of each month.

Budget Worksheet:

Monthly Pay (take-home)	Jan	Feb	Mar
Job =	$3,360		
Spouse's Job (N/A) =	$0		
Extra Job/Overtime (N/A) =	$0		
Total Income =	$3,360	$0	$0
Monthly Expenses	Jan	Feb	Mar
Entertainment	$330		
Eating Out	$188		
Miscellaneous	$45		
Credit Card #1 ($3,000 balance)	$75		
Credit Card #2 ($600 balance)	$20		
Cable TV	$125		
Cell Phone	$80		
Retirement	$92		
Discretionary Total =	$955	$0	$0
Gasoline (avg)	$210		
Car Maintenance (avg $420/yr)	$35		
Car Insurance	$80		
Car Loan ($2,000 balance)	$250		
Renter's Insurance	$50		
Rent	$600		
Dental Insurance	$125		
Health Insurance	$250		
Electric (avg)	$160		
Water (avg)	$55		
Gas (avg)	$70		
Groceries (avg)	$350		
Essential Living Total =	$2,235	$0	$0
TOTAL Expenses =	$3,190	$0	$0
Excess =	$170	$0	$0

Budget Breakdown:

- His budget is a mess - we'll fix it throughout each chapter!
- Total Income = $3,360.
- Discretionary Total = $955.
- Essential Living Total = $2,235* (see *Crisis Line below).
- Total Expenses = $3,190.
- Excess = $170.
- Debt = $5,600 total (resolve in Chapter 5).
- Emergency Fund = None (resolve in Chapter 6).
- Retirement = $92 (resolve in Chapter 7).
- House = Renting (he buys a house in Chapter 8).
- Estate Plan = None (resolve in Chapter 9).
- Insurance = car, rent, dental, health (more in Chapter 10).
- College Fund = No kids (he has one in Chapter 11).

***Crisis Line:**

The dark horizontal line on Phil's budget worksheet (in between Retirement and Gasoline) is his Crisis Line. It separates *discretionary* expenses from *essential living* expenses. The Crisis Line is very important to understand.

- Items ***below*** the line are ***essential living expenses***.

- Items ***above*** the line are ***discretionary expenses***.

Why "Crisis Line"? This line exists so that during a life

"crisis", you can immediately cut all discretionary spending *above* the line and live on the bare essentials *below* the line. This is where people can run off the rails. The definition of essential living will vary greatly depending on who you're talking to. I guess if you had to, you could live in a cardboard box under an overpass and eat table scraps from the dumpsters behind restaurants. Conversely, some folks may feel they're in a "crisis" if they have to go without the latest smart phone, laptop, daily mocha latte, or high-end luxury car. Piggy philosophy is that the line is scalable and adjustable to your current financial situation. Just because the Crisis Line is scalable, do not use that as an excuse to deem everything an essential living expense. A smart phone is NOT essential - a land line phone will work just fine, they have for decades. Cable television is NOT essential. A $350 car payment car is NOT essential. Heck, if you lived near work, a car itself may not even be essential; lots of city dwellers live without a car and bike or walk to work. Ask yourself what's essential; you'd be amazed at what you can live without during a true crisis. The Crisis Line will be referenced further in subsequent chapters.

[Notice Phil's car payment is listed as an essential living expense. That's because he needs his car to get to work. It does *not* mean it's okay to have debt or a car loan. It does *not* mean he should buy a brand new $30,000 car and deem it essential. More in Chapter 5.]

As stated earlier, this is only a SAMPLE budget. Adjust yours up/down to scale for income, expenses and placement of your Crisis Line. Do NOT use Phil's example as the "right" way to create a budget because there is no right way. Major factors such as marital status, children, incomes, housing, and more will affect your budget. Be sure to include **everything**!

Variable Expenses.

Some items on your budget will vary, such as gas, water, electric, etc. You should estimate them based upon the *average* of previous months. Example: your last 12 months water bills combined equal $720, so your average monthly expense is $60 ($720 divided by 12). Once the *actual* bill is paid for the month, enter the *actual* expense on your budget for that month. Even your income will vary over time, so adjust your budget accordingly.

Realize that YOU have much control over variable expenses. Don't let a "surprise" electric bill be an excuse not to save for retirement that month. You can be extremely accurate when averaging expenses over a 12-month period. Also, turning off lights and televisions when not in a room and adjusting your thermostat for minimal use when not at home will make a big difference in your bill. You pay for what you USE, not what the utility company decides to charge. Also, this applies to discretionary items such as entertainment, eating out, movies, etc.

Your budget should be **categorized**, **prioritized** and **proportioned**.

Categorize.

When categorizing expenses, find a reasonable balance. For example, you would not want an expense called "utilities" that lumps water, electric, and gas all into a single expense. That expense would not only fluctuate too much, but would be difficult to budget properly each month. Conversely, you don't want 200 rows of expenses on your budget worksheet (i.e. milk, eggs, butter, cereal, etc). These could more appropriately be tracked as "groceries". A category such as "entertainment" may work, but if you find 80% of that expense is consistently going out to the movies, you may want to add a separate expense for "movies" and keep the rest in "entertainment". You'll get comfortable with what works for you after a few months of budgeting. Remember, every dollar gets tracked! Although other things are a mess, Phil's budget is *categorized* fairly well.

Prioritize.

Expenses on your budget must be prioritized, listing which to pay first. Focus on major items only. Don't stress over non-sense. Is the electric bill really more important than the water bill, or vice versa? No. If it is, you're in serious trouble. Prioritizing allows you to pay the most essential items first, working your way up to the least essential. If you're low on money one month, it will be easy to cut out non-essential items. In alignment with the piggy principles, here's a prioritization of major expenses. Items on bottom are paid before items on top:

Pay **Last** --> #7 - Disposable (play money)
　　　　　　　 #6 - College Fund (if applicable)
　　　　　　　 #5 - Mortgage (if applicable)
　　　　　　　 #4 - Retirement (10% of take-home pay)
　　　　　　　 #3 - Emergency Fund (6-months of expenses)
　　　　　　　 #2 - Debt (100% debt-free, except house)
Pay **First** --> **#1 - Essential Living Expenses**

But wait a minute...you pay your mortgage (#5) *after* your credit cards (#2)?! No, that's not how it works - let me explain. If you already have a mortgage, it's part of your essential living expenses (#1). However, if you follow the piggy philosophy, you will not buy a house (mortgage) until you are completely debt free (#2), have a full emergency fund (#3), and are saving 10% of your income for retirement (#4). We'll discuss more in those chapters.

So, compare this *prioritization* to Phil's budget:

#7 - He wastes money while in debt; prioritized wrong; resolve in Chapter 5.
#6 - Not applicable ($0); he has no kids; he will in Chapter 11.
#5 - Not applicable ($0); he rents; buys a house in Chapter 8.
#4 - He saves $92 for retirement; too little; prioritized wrong; resolve in Chapter 7.
#3 - No Emergency Fund; prioritized wrong; resolve in Chapter 6.
#2 - He has $5,600 in Debt; prioritized wrong; resolve in Chapter 5.
#1 - He pays his living expenses first; prioritized correctly.

Proportion.

When proportioning your budget, the goal is to ensure your income and major expenses are balanced in relation to each other. **The Golden Rule is that Total Income must always be more than Total Expenses.** Again, just like in prioritization, you only proportion major expenses; when it comes to proportion, don't stress out over every dollar. Here are some rules of thumb for major expenses:

House
- 25% of take-home pay, maximum (rent or mortgage)
- Budget taxes, insurance & maintenance separately
- More in Chapter 8

Retirement
- 10% of take-home pay, minimum (15% maximum)
- More in Chapter 7

Vehicle
- 5% of take-home pay, max. Ideally, pay cash.
- 3-year loan maximum; always with 20% down
- More in Chapter 5

How well is Phil's budget *proportioned*?

Total Income > Total Expenses
- He's cutting it close, but passes the test!

House
- 25% of take-home pay is $840; his rent is $600 - he's okay!

Retirement
- 10% of take-home pay is $336; he saves $92 - not enough!

Vehicle
- His car loan is $250/mo; no good - his retirement's at risk!

That is the magic of your budget - you get to actually SEE where your money goes every month. Ideally, you should have money left over at the end of the month - if not, you need to figure out why; not enough income, too much spending, etc. You'll notice the "excess amount" will vary each month because your *income* may vary and/or, most surely, your *expenses* will vary. As you can see, a budget is a useful tool and has many benefits...

- Allows you to spend money *where* & *how* you want!
- Helps to keep you from spending more than you make.
- Gives you financial peace of mind!

Additionally, when it comes to the core components of your financial house of brick, your **budget** has 6 superpowers that enable you to...

- Eliminate **debt**.
- Build your **emergency fund**.
- Fund your **retirement**.
- Afford your **house**.
- Manage your **estate plan**.
- Adjust your **insurance** needs.

When it comes to budgeting, some people can become frustrated when trying to set money goals. Whether you're trying to pay off debt, increase earnings, or save more money, it helps to start with SMART goals. The acronym SMART is often used in management circles and has slightly variable meanings, depending on the environment. To help improve your finances, you should set money goals that are SMART.

S - Specific. Goals should be well defined and focused. "Paying off my credit card" is more specific than "paying down my debt". Do not set vague goals.

M - Measurable. A goal that can't be measured is doomed to failure. "Increasing next year's earnings by $2,000" is measurable. "Earning more money" is not.

A - Achievable. Is your goal attainable? If you earn $50K/year, then paying off $55K in debt this year is probably not achievable. Don't set yourself up for failure.

R - Relevant. Is your goal relevant, or related to your long-term strategy? If you plan to become an engineer, then setting a goal to earn an bachelor's degree in engineering is relevant (a degree in history is not).

T - Time-based. Goals should be time-specific. "Paying off my credit card by June 1st" is time-specific. "Paying off my credit card soon" is not.

Even with SMART goals, you may still have trouble sticking to your "money diet". In this case, you should start small and work your way up. Set small, easy goals in order to build your confidence. For example, suppose you owe $7,500 on a credit card and you're only making the minimum payment each month. You might want to set a SMART goal of "Pay an extra $50 per month on my credit card for the next 6 months". The extra $50 each month may not seem like a lot, but it will reinforce your ability to meet goals and also reduce your credit card balance by an extra $300. Once you get the hang of budgeting, you'll be a pro in no time!

So, you know what a budget is, how to create one, and the many benefits it offers. You also know when budgeting, you should set money goals that are SMART. A budget forms the foundation of your financial house and will be referenced again many more times. You'll see how the budget helps you build each and every component of your financial house. Since we've built a solid foundation, it's now time to ensure our house stays nice and dry and does not get destroyed by a rising cesspool of debt.

KEY TAKEAWAYS
- A budget is a written plan on how to spend your income.
- Your budget must be:
    - categorized
    - prioritized
    - proportioned
- Golden Rule: total income > total expenses
- Crisis Line: separates discretionary & living expenses
- Living expenses: required to live; items below the crisis line.
- Discretionary expenses: items not required to live; items above the crisis line.
- Total expenses = living expenses + discretionary expenses.
- Budget benefits:
    - Allows you to spend money *where* & *how* you want!
    - Helps to keep you from spending more than you make.
    - Gives you financial peace of mind.
- Your budget's 6 superpowers:
    - Eliminate debt.
    - Build your emergency fund.
    - Fund your retirement.
    - Afford your house.
    - Manage your estate plan.
    - Adjust your insurance needs.
- When budgeting, set SMART money goals.

"A budget is telling your money where to go instead of wondering where it went." -John Maxwell

CHAPTER 5
DEBT (BASEMENT)

Oh, that nasty, 4-letter word! Let's face it, when it comes to *debt*, most of us want to hide it, bury it, or sweep it under the rug as if it doesn't exist. That's why we place debt in the basement of our financial house. The basement is where dead bodies get hidden, rats build their homes, and even where the Amityville Horror House demon lived! Heck, why not just put our debt in the basement too? Why? Because this rich little piggy is building a financial house of brick! Your basement must be a clean, dry, finished living space. Living debt free is piggy principle #3.

1. Grow your income
2. Follow a written budget
3. **Live debt free**
4. Build a 6-month emergency fund
5. Save 10% of income for retirement
6. Pay it forward

For little piggy purposes, unless specified otherwise, debt-free means everything except your house. That means *everything* except the house; it includes car loans, student loans, boats, motorcycles, credit cards, etc. House debt (mortgage) will be discussed further in Chapter 8. Using our newly created budget, we're going to ensure we get debt free and stay debt free. This must also happen before we build our emergency fund. See piggy pay priority below. Not surprisingly, becoming debt free can be extremely difficult.

Pay **Last** --> #7 - Disposable (play money)
　　　　　　　#6 - College Fund (if applicable)
　　　　　　　#5 - Mortgage (if applicable)
　　　　　　　#4 - Retirement (10% of take-home pay)
　　　　　　　#3 - Emergency Fund (6-months of expenses)
　　　　　　　#2 - Debt (100% debt-free, except house)
Pay **First** --> #1 - Essential Living Expenses

The trick to becoming debt free is to not get into debt in the first place! Funny, right? You're kidding, right? No, not really. Sadly, our nation is one of debt; mortgage debt, automobile debt, student loan debt, credit card debt, payday loans, 401K loans, home equity loans, medical debt, weddings ('til debt do us part), and seemingly endless other debts. If you follow the herd, you know where you'll end up. Are you keeping up with the Joneses? Those darn Joneses! Are you worshipping possessions over people? Avoiding these debt landmines is no easy feat. It involves being able to recognize the risk, understanding how to get out of the situation, and ultimately, learning how never to go back into it. There are subtle differences in avoiding debt, getting out of debt, and staying out of debt. So, before learning how to **get out of debt** and then **stay out of debt**, it's important to avoid it by first reflecting on **how we get into debt in the first place**.

How do so many people get into debt in the first place? How many of us are issued a credit card along with our birth certificate? Are we born with debt? Do we get it buying school supplies? Does it come as a package deal when we get our high school diploma? How about buying our first car? Paying for college? Where do we first lose our debt-free virginity? Well, your guess is as good as anyone's! Here's my guess - **people don't follow a written budget!** There are untold ways that people first get into debt, just look around you. The challenge is to prevent YOURSELF from getting into debt. Interestingly enough, that is not so much a *money* issue as it is a *self-discipline* issue (*values* and *behavior*). This goes back to the character values of our piggy philosophy and our income. While there's no need to re-iterate what's already been said in our piggy philosophy, it must be mentioned here that following the philosophy is very much a part of *how* to live debt free. Even more so than some mathematical debt-free formula, a rags-to-riches secret or a magical infomercial how-to process. You can't follow *some* of it or *part* of it and expect to be successful - it doesn't work that way. Your character values must be not only words, but they must also drive your every day *actions* if you truly desire to live a rich, debt-free life. Starting out in life, the sooner you start producing income (working), the quicker and farther you'll distance yourself from life's debt demons. Let's take a look at one of life's typical "rights of passage" as an example of how easily people can fall into debt.

What teenager doesn't dream of having their own car? A car is a prime example of how people first get into debt, so let's use it as just one valuable teaching moment. Those pesky cars come with a thirst for gasoline, oil, maintenance, and a security blanket called insurance, all of which cost money. If you can pay cash for a car, then no worries. However, if your financial house is not yet in order, here are some general rules when considering a vehicle...

- Is it required right now? If you can carpool, bike, or walk until you can pay cash, then do so.
- If required right now for work, buy the least expensive (yet reliable) vehicle possible. Put down as *much* & borrow as *little* as possible; a *maximum* loan of 3 years!
- Do NOT talk yourself into buying over your head! You must go from point A to point B. Leather seats, sunroof, and DVD package are NOT required.
- Plan and budget for gas, fluids, insurance, and periodic maintenance.

If you follow these general car buying rules, you'll be fine. Even as a teenager, taking on a part-time job will allow you to stash away money towards your first car. Trust me, you'll be able to drive whatever you like later on. Sadly, a car is but just one way that people first fall into debt. We could fill a library with countless other examples, but that's unnecessary (and causes migraines), so we won't go there. The underlying premise is to buy only what you *need*. The *niceties* will come later in life, once you've built a solid financial house. Ok, unfortunately, you were never shown how to live like a rich little piggy until now and so, despite your best efforts to avoid debt, the unthinkable has already happened...you're in debt. Now what? Now...you must get out, that's what.

Getting out of debt is far more difficult (and painful) than not getting into debt in the first place. Avoiding the quicksand can be tricky, but getting out of it, wow, that's the tough part. But now that you're there, this is one of those times to get serious! That's right, not kinda serious, not sorta serious, or even kinda-sorta serious...you know it by now, HOG WILD serious! The toughest hurdle to living the rich piggy lifestyle is getting out of debt. However, once you conquer this, you'll be able to conquer anything! You're drowning, you're suffocating, and that cesspool of debt is threatening every breath you take. How badly do you want to get out of debt? Maybe? It's not so bad? Then close the book and go charge some mocha lattes on your credit card while shopping at the mall. But when you're finally sick and tired of gulping sewage, and you're ready to start living, it's time to break the shackles of debt. How? By following the 3-step piggy process outlined below.

First, you must stop the bleeding. ***Second***, close your credit lines. ***Lastly***, use the debt pyramid to eliminate your debt. Following the first step is undoubtedly the most difficult.

Debt Elimination Process:
1. Stop the bleeding (no additional debt)
2. Cut up credit cards (close credit lines)
3. Debt pyramid (stack smallest to largest; pay smallest first)

STEP 1. (Stop Bleeding) The first piggy step to getting out of debt is to *stop the bleeding*. This means you will not incur any additional debt; not one single dollar more. Enough is enough. There are basically two sub-steps in this process.

STEP 1.a. (Apply Tourniquet) This sub-step involves your budget, remember that? As stated earlier, one of the 6 superpowers that your budget will enable you to do is *eliminate debt*. Since you've already built a budget worksheet (the foundation of your financial house), you've made this sub-step a lot easier on yourself. You'll open your budget and slash every expense above the Crisis Line. Remember the Crisis Line, from Chapter 4?

[exception: continue minimum payments on loans and credit cards if you can afford to.]

But what about contributing to retirement, you ask? What about cable television and top-of-the-line smart phone data plans? What about the kid's college fund for crying out loud? Right now, they don't matter - that's what. You're in debt and being in debt is an **emergency**! You're going to cut back on everything except essential living expenses (those items below the Crisis Line on your budget). You may have to sell stuff, including blood. It's about getting HOG WILD folks. Spending the same way you've been spending to get yourself into debt will NOT get you out of debt. You must make drastic changes. You and debt go into a room, lock the door, pull down the blinds and shutter the windows; only *one* of you is walking out! This is not a game. Luckily, the next sub-step can be worked simultaneously with the first.

STEP 1.b. (Boost Income) This sub-step requires you to kick in the after-burners, put it in overdrive, or initiate warp speed, depending on your cup of tea. That means boosting your income! You can boost your income by requesting overtime at your job. If your boss will not authorize overtime, then you need to take a part-time job. Heck, take TWO part-time jobs. Whatever it takes. It doesn't matter what the job is; cashier, fast food, pizza delivery, security guard, mowing lawns or whatever is available. If your spouse is not working, it's time for them to start looking. Just be sure the job covers the cost of daycare if you have children. Maybe you have family that will temporarily serve as your 'daycare'? It's time to exhaust all avenues of boosting your income. The basement is filling with raw sewage and you need as many buckets as possible to start bailing. Once you've cut expenses and started earning more money, you then move to the second step.

STEP 2. (Close Credit) The second piggy step in the debt elimination process is *cut up your credit cards and close out credit lines.* Why is this not the first step? Because if you're in debt, you're either spending more than you earn every month and/or you're cutting is so tight that you barely have any room for error. Defaulting on payments unnecessarily is not smart. Once you have slashed spending and increased your income (step 1), you can feel a lot more confident about closing down credit lines and never using them ever again!

First, if you don't have one already, get a *debit* card - preferably one with a MasterCard or Visa logo, or other major credit company. A *debit* card with a major credit company logo does not extend you *credit*. You can not charge things on a debit card. Instead, it links directly to your bank account, where you keep your money. When you swipe your debit card at the store, the money is deducted from your bank account, just like writing a check. This means you can't buy anything unless you have the cash in the bank! A debit card with a major credit logo offers the same consumer protection as an ordinary credit card. You can use it at gas stations and stores just like you would a credit card, except that you must have the money in your bank account (no credit). No minimum monthly payments, no interest, late fees, penalties, annual fees, headaches, or debt!

Once you have your debit card in place, you can call the bank and have them close all of your *credit* card accounts. You'll still be required to pay off the remaining balance, but you'll be unable to charge any more expenses. This includes department store cards, gas cards, and any other credit card you may have. You can then (with a big smile) cut up your credit cards and toss them in the trash. If you have any open lines of credit, you will close them down also. This includes home equity lines, personal loans, and any other source of credit. Now, you're ready for the final debt elimination step.

STEP 3. (Debt Pyramid) The third and final piggy step in the debt elimination process is to use the ***debt pyramid***. You will list all of your debts from smallest to largest, placing the smallest at the top and largest at the bottom. [See example debt pyramid figure]. If you have a mortgage, do not include it in this process; it will be addressed in Chapter 8. The term 'largest' means the debt with the biggest *balance* still owed; it does not mean the largest monthly payment. For example, if you have a credit card with a $3,000 balance, you may have a $75 minimum payment. You may also have a car loan with a remaining balance of $2,000, but the monthly payment is $250. In this example, the credit card loan is the 'largest'. The largest debt forms the base (bottom) of your pyramid. The next smallest debt goes on top of that, and so on, leaving the smallest debt you have at the top of the pyramid. Whether you have one debt or many, it does not matter, follow the same procedure.

Also, the interest rate does not matter unless both debts are the same amount. For example, if you had 2 credit cards with balances of $2,000 on each, one with a 7% interest rate, and one with a 12% interest rate, the one with a 12% interest rate would go on top of the one with the 7% interest rate. However, the credit card with the $2,000 balance (12% interest rate) would still go *under* (below) a credit card with a $1,000 balance (no matter the interest rate). Once your debt pyramid is complete, you will continue paying the *minimum* payment required on every single debt. However, you will pay as much as humanly possible on the top debt (the smallest). Remember, you have slashed every non-essential expense from your budget and have boosted your income by working like crazy. Every spare dollar you have will go to pay on that top debt. You do not have a life until your debt is gone. When the top debt is finally paid off, you will continue doing the same for the next smallest debt, but this time you will also include the payment that you were paying on the first (top) debt and so on, until every single debt is paid off. Here's an example...

All Debts (Example, Debt Pyramid)

Balance	Min Payment	Item
$3,000	$75	credit card
$4,000	$100	boat loan
$5,000	$200	car loan
$12,000	$400	student loan
$24,000	**$775**	**TOTAL**

In this example, you will pay the *minimum* payment for all debts (total of $775). Also, every extra dollar you have for the month will go towards the credit card, in addition to the $75 minimum payment. If you have $100 dollars left over at the end of the month, guess what? Every penny of that $100 does towards the credit card.

Once the credit card is paid off, you will continue paying the minimum payment for all remaining debts, now a total of $700. The $75 that you *were* paying to the credit card will now get applied to the boat loan, in addition to its minimum payment of $100. Also, every extra dollar you have for the month will now go towards the boat loan. Continue this pattern until all debts are paid in full.

Phil Attacks His Debt!

Since Phil T. Pig has $5,600 in debt, let's apply the above Debt Elimination Process to Phil's budget. To refresh our memory, let's look at his financial status again:

Financial Status:

Financial Component	Status
Income	Started; Growing
Budget	Complete
Debt	$5,600 total
Emergency Fund	Chapter 6
Retirement	Chapter 7
House	Chapter 8
Estate Plan	Chapter 9
Insurance	Chapter 10
College Fund	Chapter 11

Keep in mind that Phil currently has three debts. He has two credit cards, one with a balance of $3,000 and the other with a balance of $600. His other debt is his car loan, which has a balance of $2,000. All together, these debts are costing Phil $345 per month; that's with making only minimum payments.

Let's take a closer look at Phil's current budget. You'll notice his three debts are shaded in gray and **bold**.

Phil's current budget (3 debts highlighted in gray & **bold**):

Monthly Pay (take-home)	Jan	Feb	Mar
Job =	$3,360		
Spouse's Job (N/A) =	$0		
Extra Job/Overtime (N/A) =	$0		
Total Income =	$3,360	$0	$0
Monthly Expenses	Jan	Feb	Mar
Entertainment	$330		
Eating Out	$188		
Miscellaneous	$45		
Credit Card #1 ($3,000)	$75		
Credit Card #2 ($600 balance)	$20		
Cable TV	$125		
Cell Phone	$80		
Retirement	$92		
Discretionary Total =	$955	$0	$0
Gasoline (avg)	$210		
Car Maintenance (avg $420/yr)	$35		
Car Insurance	$80		
Car Loan ($2,000 balance)	$250		
Renter's Insurance	$50		
Rent	$600		
Dental Insurance	$125		
Health Insurance	$250		
Electric (avg)	$160		
Water (avg)	$55		
Gas (avg)	$70		
Groceries (avg)	$350		
Essential Living Total =	$2,235	$0	$0
TOTAL Expenses =	$3,190	$0	$0
Excess =	$170	$0	$0

(Phil T. Pig) Step 1.a. (Apply Tourniquet). The first thing Phil does is stop spending everything above his Crisis Line. That will save him $860/month as shown below.

[note: since he can still afford his living expenses, he'll keep making minimum payments on the 2 credit cards: $75 & $20 each.]

Monthly Savings (cut discretionary items).

Average	Expense	What Now?
$330	Entertainment	Work more (side-job / OT)
$188	Eating Out	Eat In
$45	Misc	Tighten your belt
$125	Cable TV	Too broke/busy to watch TV
$80	Cell Phone	Use a land-line (it works)
$92	Retirement	On hold; debt emergency
$860	**Total Savings**	**Pay towards debt pyramid!**

(Phil T. Pig) Step 1.b. (Boost Income). Phil picks up a part-time job to earn an extra $200/month. Remember, he also has $170 "excess" in his budget and an extra $860 from above. All of this gets combined to be thrown at his debt as shown below.

Extra	Source	What Now?
$860	Cut discretionary items	Pay towards debt pyramid!
$200	Part-time job	Pay towards debt pyramid!
$170	Excess budget money	Pay towards debt pyramid!
$1,230	**Total Extra**	**Pay towards debt pyramid!**

(Phil T. Pig) Step 2. (Close Credit). Phil calls his credit card companies and tells them to close the accounts. He then (with a smile) cuts them up. The balances are paid off in Step 3.

(Phil T. Pig) Step 3. (Debt Pyramid). He lists his debts from smallest to largest, as shown below.

Debt Pyramid (Starting Point)

Balance	Min Payment	Item
$600	$20	Credit Card #2
$2,000	$250	Car Loan
$3,000	$75	Credit Card #1
$5,600	**$345**	**TOTAL**

Step 1 gave Phil an extra $1,230. He applies $580 of it (plus the original $20 minimum payment he's already budgeted) to his smallest debt first (Credit Card #2). That pays it in full and leaves $650 ($1,230 - $580) to apply to his second largest debt (Car Loan).

The remaining $650 plus the $250 minimum payment on the Car Loan gives him $900 to apply toward the balance, bringing it down to $1,100. Phil also makes the $75 minimum payment on Credit Card #1. After one month of the Debt Elimination Process, take a look at the updated debt pyramid.

Debt Pyramid (After 1 Month)

Balance	Min Payment	Item
$0	$0	Credit Card #2
$1,100	$250	Car Loan
$2,925	$75	Credit Card #1
$4,025	**$325**	**TOTAL**

You can easily see that Credit Card #2 is paid in full and his car loan is significantly lower. Also, Credit Card #1 is lower because Phil made the $75 minimum payment.

So, before we continue with month 2 of Phil's Debt Pyramid, let's pause and see what his budget would actually look like after the first month.

After 1 month of debt pyramid; updates in gray & **bold**.

Monthly Pay (take-home)	Jan	Feb	Mar
Job =	$3,360	$3,360	
Spouse's Job (N/A) =	$0	$0	
Extra Job/Overtime (N/A) =	$0	**$200**	
Total Income =	$3,360	$3,560	$0
Monthly Expenses	Jan	Feb	Mar
Entertainment	$330	**$0**	
Eating Out	$188	**$0**	
Miscellaneous	$45	**$0**	
Credit Card #1 ($2,925)	$75	$75	
Credit Card #2 ($0 balance)	$20	**$600**	
Cable TV	$125	**$0**	
Cell Phone	$80	**$0**	
Retirement	$92	**$0**	
Discretionary Total =	$955	$675	$0
Gasoline (avg)	$210	$210	
Car Maintenance (avg $420/yr)	$35	$35	
Car Insurance	$80	$80	
Car Loan ($1,100 balance)	$250	**$900**	
Renter's Insurance	$50	$50	
Rent	$600	$600	
Dental Insurance	$125	$125	
Health Insurance	$250	$250	
Electric (avg)	$160	$160	
Water (avg)	$55	$55	
Gas (avg)	$70	$70	
Groceries (avg)	$350	$350	
Essential Living Total =	$2,235	$2,885	$0
TOTAL Expenses =	$3,190	$3,560	$0
Excess =	$170	$0	$0

Notice a few things on Phil's budget while he's working the Debt Pyramid:

- He's earning $200/mo extra at his part-time job.
- Discretionary spending is temporarily $0 (zero).
- Every spare dollar goes towards the debt pyramid.

So, let's continue on to month 2 of the Debt Pyramid. Phil applies another $1,230 (plus the $20 that he *was* paying towards Credit Card #2), plus the $250 minimum payment for the car = Total $1,500. Since the car balance is only $1,100, it's now paid in full and he applies the remaining $400 to his regular $75 Credit Card #1 payment ($475 total). See what it looks like below.

Debt Pyramid (After 2 Months)

Balance	Min Payment	Item
$0	$0	Credit Card #2
$0	$0	Car Loan
$2,450	$75	Credit Card #1
$2,450	**$75**	**TOTAL**

Phil now takes the $1,230 (plus the $20 he *was* paying towards Credit Card #2 and the $250 he *was* paying to the car) and the $75 regular Credit Card #1 payment = Total $1,575. Let's see what his debt pyramid looks like now (after just 3 months)!

Debt Pyramid (After 3 Months)

Balance	Min Payment	Item
$0	$0	Credit Card #2
$0	$0	Car Loan
$875	$75	Credit Card #1
$875	**$75**	**TOTAL**

Phil now takes the $1,230 (plus the $20 he *was* paying towards the Credit Card #2 and the $250 he *was* paying to the car) and the $75 regular Credit Card #1 payment = Total $1,575. Since the balance is only $875, he has $700 left over for discretionary spending again.

Debt Pyramid (After 4 months)

Balance	Min Payment	Item
$0	$0	Credit Card #2
$0	$0	Car Loan
$0	$0	Credit Card #1
$0	**$0**	**TOTAL**

Phil's budget for the month of May, after just *4 months* of his Debt Pyramid would look as follows.

Updates in gray & **bold**. He is now **DEBT FREE!**

Monthly Pay (take-home)	Mar	Apr	May
Job =	$3,360	$3,360	$3,360
Spouse's Job (N/A) =	$0	$0	$0
Extra Job/Overtime (N/A) =	$200	$200	**$200**
Total Income =	$3,560	$3,560	$3,560
Monthly Expenses	Mar	Apr	May
Entertainment	$0	$0	$0
Eating Out	$0	$0	$0
Miscellaneous	$0	$0	$0
Credit Card #1 ($0 balance)	$475	$1,575	**$875**
Credit Card #2 ($0 balance)	$0	$0	$0
Cable TV	$0	$0	$0
Cell Phone	$0	$0	$0
Retirement	$0	$0	$0
Discretionary Total =	$475	$1,575	$875
Gasoline (avg)	$210	$210	$210
Car Maintenance (avg $420/yr)	$35	$35	$35
Car Insurance	$80	$80	$80
Car Loan ($0 balance)	$1,100	$0	$0
Renter's Insurance	$50	$50	$50
Rent	$600	$600	$600
Dental Insurance	$125	$125	$125
Health Insurance	$250	$250	$250
Electric (avg)	$160	$160	$160
Water (avg)	$55	$55	$55
Gas (avg)	$70	$70	$70
Groceries (avg)	$350	$350	$350
Essential Living Total =	$3,085	$1,985	$1,985
TOTAL Expenses =	$3,560	$3,560	**$2,860**
Excess =	$0	$0	**$700**

Notice a few things on Phil's budget now that he's finished his Debt Pyramid:

- He still earns $200/mo extra (part-time job).
- Discretionary spending may resume next month.
- He has $700 "Excess" this month - time to party!
- His 3 debts will drop off his budget next month.

Ok, so you know how people fall into debt in the first place and some ways to avoid falling into it yourself. And, if unfortunately you're already in debt, you now know how to get out of it. We saw first-hand through Phil's experience how painful it can be, but he somehow survived. Phew! This debt thing can be a serious headache, so how do we stay out of it?

Knowing **how to stay out of debt** is half the battle - actually doing it is the other half! There are two strategies that will help you stay out of debt:

- Following the 4 Debt Don'ts
- Pre-Funding major planned expenses

DEBT DON'Ts:
#1 - NEVER co-sign a loan for ANYONE!
#2 - NEVER take out a payday or title loan!
#3 - NEVER use an unsecured credit card!
#4 - NEVER borrow from your retirement!

It's not good enough to simply know the 4 Debt Don'ts, but you should also tattoo them on your forearm. No, don't, just kidding. However, be sure to actually *follow* them and also understand *why* they're Debt Don'ts. To add some understanding, let's look at each one a little closer.

#1 - NEVER co-sign a loan for ANYONE!

To begin with, you must understand that co-signing a loan for someone is not simply vouching for their integrity or their ability to pay back the loan. When you co-sign a loan, you are taking out the loan right along with them! If the person taking out the loan does not pay it back, YOU will. If the person dies, guess who's responsible for the loan? You guessed it! If the person is late making payments, guess whose credit suffers? Bingo! If it's too late and you've already co-signed a loan, you should ask the person to refinance in their name only. If enough time has passed on the original loan, they may now be eligible to refinance without a co-signer because they've since built up enough credit or the loan balance is now substantially lower. You may be fully confident that the person you co-signed for would not miss a payment if their life depended on it. Well, what if that person dies? Who makes the payments then? If you can't get off a loan that you co-signed for, depending on how much it is, you should consider taking out a life insurance policy against the primary borrower. For example, you co-signed for $65,000 in student loans for your daughter. If the unthinkable happens and your daughter passes away before you, then the co-signer (YOU) will be fully responsible for the entire balance on the loans.

#2 - NEVER take out a payday or title loan!

Payday and title loans are both short-term, HIGH interest loans. In the case of payday loans, the lender is giving you a cash advance (typically $500-$1,000) and you pay it back when you get your paycheck. They require a personal check or bank account access before giving you the money; that ensures they'll get paid, with interest and fees, of course. Suffice it to say, payday loans have astronomical interest rates!

Title loans operate in a similar fashion, but instead of borrowing against your next paycheck, you give the lender the title to your vehicle (car, motorcycle, etc). When you pay them back, with interest and fees, you get your title back.

If you manage your finances properly and have even a minimal emergency fund, there will never be a need for a payday or title loan - ever! The exorbitant interest rates and finance fees will lead to a vicious borrowing cycle that will leave you addicted to more loans and drowning in debt.

#3 - NEVER use an unsecured credit card!

Unsecured credit card? Huh? Some people tell us credit cards are evil and they should never, ever be used. They say we should cut them up and throw them away - use debit or cash only. That's mostly true. Other people will tell us to use credit cards responsibly because it will help us build our credit score - we're told we must all worship our credit scores. A little true. Well, I say do neither. Or both, depending on how you look at it. There are many different types of cards offered by banks and one 'hybrid' offers the benefits of each. Here's a quick snapshot of each type.

The **traditional (unsecured) credit card** is where you require a good credit score to qualify and the bank extends you credit on your card. When you buy something on the card, the bank "loans" you the money and you agree to pay it back. If you pay it in full every month, there are *normally* no interest charges or fees, depending on the terms of your card. Proper use of a credit card will help boost your credit score. The downside is that most people will not pay it off in full every month and steadily run up a huge amount of debt, not to mention interest charges. Never use this kind of card.

A **debit card** does not extend you any credit (even the ones with a major credit company logo). It simply links to your bank account. So, every time you buy something with your debit card, the money is automatically deducted from your bank account, just like writing a check. For people who can not control their spending, a debit card is a great choice. The downside is that you'll miss an opportunity to build your credit score. I'll take zero debt over a good credit score any day! A debit card is a good choice, but in my opinion, the next one is better.

A **secured credit card** is sort of a 'hybrid' solution that offers the best of both worlds. How does it work? You give the bank an amount of money equal to your desired 'credit line', just say $1,000. The bank holds that money in your account, thus **securing** you a credit card with a $1,000 limit. This is no different than having money in your checking or savings account. You can then buy items just as you would by using a traditional, unsecured, credit card, up to $1,000. *Unlike* a debit card, your secured credit card spending *does* get reported to the credit bureaus. So, if you pay your bill faithfully, you can help build your credit score. But *like* a debit card, you must have the money in the bank in order to spend it. Thus, just like paying cash. In a nutshell, you pay cash but build credit.

There are even prepaid debit and prepaid credit cards available at most banks. Be sure to do your research and carefully read the terms of each before committing to any card. You do not want to be surprised by annual fees, high interest rates, or any other fine print.

#4 - NEVER borrow from your retirement!

This one might be a tough one for some people. I can't tell you how many horror stories I hear about people having a life "emergency" and tapping into their retirement accounts for quick cash. A big no-no! You can "what if" this one all day long, but unless it is practically life or death, there are very few reasons to ever borrow from your retirement account. Like most piggy principles, I always like to go a bit deeper and explain my thoughts on why. In this situation, there are two main reasons you should never borrow from your retirement.

The first reason not to borrow from your retirement account is because you'll get nailed with penalties and taxes. With few exceptions, you'll pay applicable federal and state income taxes, plus a 10% penalty on the amount you withdraw. Yeah, yeah, you won't owe any of this because you'll pay it back - uh, huh. Famous last words. Typically, the maximum loan term is 5 years. However, if you lose your job with that employer, the loan is usually due paid in full within 2 months - now what? Oh by the way, you originally put your money into your retirement account *before* tax. When you pay the money back from a loan, it's paid back *after* tax. Then, you get to pay taxes *again* when you withdraw it in retirement. A Roth IRA is different and, under qualified circumstances, you can withdraw money without taxes and penalty. However, that is a big negative for the Roth. People are going to be tempted to use their retirement account as a piggy-bank and never get to retire. For the most part, your money must be in the Roth for at least 5 years before you can avoid the taxes. Ok, enough about taxes and penalties because there are countless rules and exceptions to follow. Consult your tax attorney if you ever think about borrowing from your retirement account. After that, consult your bartender! So, if that's not enough, there's one more reason not to borrow from your retirement account.

The second reason not to borrow from your retirement is that you're only treating the *symptom*, not the *cause* of your financial emergency. If you're following the principles, there should rarely ever be a need to borrow from your retirement account. With rare exception, borrowing from your retirement will not permanently fix anything. In fact, it usually makes the situation worse. You might fix a temporary problem now, but you sacrifice your future retirement in doing so. You're borrowing from tomorrow to pay for today. Besides, what would you do if you had no money in your retirement account to borrow? What would you do then? Well, in most cases, that's exactly what you should do now. Act like you don't have the money and it will still be there for you in retirement. Don't make a short-term decision for a long-term problem.

Pre-Funding:

In addition to following the 4 Debt Don'ts, pre-funding is another method used to stay out of debt. By using pre-funding, you simply save up for major planned expenses. This is where your budget is critical. After all, it's the foundation of your financial brick house and you'll be reviewing it at least once a month. We all have planned expenses in life; vacations, weddings, new car, house, etc. Planned expenses are generally 'big ticket' items. While we can't always pay cash for a house, pre-funding will help minimize borrowing. Smaller items are already budgeted for; entertainment, eating out, movies, etc. However, if you plan on a big ticket expense, you should pre-fund it. After all, most cars don't last forever, so planning on a new one at some point is probably a good idea. With a little planning and forethought into these expenses you can pre-fund them by budgeting for them each month. For example, how much are you currently saving each month for a car? News flash - your current one won't last forever. How much are you saving for a down payment on a house? You should determine, based upon your budget, how much money you'll need to save each month to afford a new car, or have a down payment on a house. You're the Chief Financial Officer of your life; at times, you'll have to make the tough call and decide which is more important, car or house, wedding or vacation. After all, most likely you're not in Congress, so you can't spend money you don't have and hope someone will pay for it later.

So, you can see that debt is no fun. Although you have a Debt Elimination Process to follow, sometimes that's not enough. If your debt is extremely severe, you may require professional credit counseling or a bankruptcy attorney. There are some credit counseling agencies listed in Appendix C if you feel they're necessary. If you choose to pursue this route, do your homework first. Some counseling approaches have the potential to make a bad situation worse by treating the symptom (debt) instead of the root cause (not enough income and/or reckless spending). That's how people end up filing multiple bankruptcies over their lifetime. If all else fails, consult a bankruptcy attorney. Just be prepared for a long, ugly, and painful process.

You should only stop your debt elimination process under two conditions. The *first*, is when you're complete; when you've paid off all debt except your house. The *second*, is if you have an actual emergency, in which case you put your debt payments on hold until the emergency is resolved, and then resume saving again.

In honor of living debt free, and speaking tongue-in-cheek, I've declared January 8th to be National Debt Free Day! My off-the-cuff research shows that Jan 8, 1835 was the only day in history that the United States was debt free. Depending on what research you believe, it was President Andrew Jackson who paid off the last installment of $33,733. Supposedly, being debt free did not last more than a year and only got worse since then. Oh well. So, to have a little fun with it, I encourage everyone to use January 8th as a day to kick-off their quest to live debt free! If only Congress would do the same.

In addition to getting out of debt and staying out of debt, life's unexpected surprises must also be budgeted for. That brings us to, by far, one of the most important things you can do to stay out of debt - establish an emergency fund.

KEY TAKEAWAYS
- Start paying off debt *after* you:
    - Create your budget.
- Debt free includes all debt, except your house.
- Get out of debt; use the Debt Elimination Process:
    - Step 1. Stop the bleeding.
        - Step 1.a. Apply tourniquet.
        - Step 1.b Boost income.
    - Step 2. Close credit.
    - Step 3. Debt Pyramid.
        - Stack debt, smallest to largest.
        - Pay smallest first until complete.
- Stay out of debt!
    - Follow the 4 Debt Don'ts
        - #1 - NEVER co-sign a loan for ANYONE!
        - #2 - NEVER take out a payday or title loan!
        - #3 - NEVER use an unsecured credit card!
        - #4 - NEVER borrow from your retirement!
    - Use Pre-funding for major planned expenses.
- Consider counseling or bankruptcy for severe debt issues.
- Celebrate National Debt Free Day (Jan 8th)!

"Your career is your business. It's time for you to manage it as a CEO." -Dorit Sher

David W. Robbins

CHAPTER 6
EMERGENCY FUND (PILLAR)

Once you've built a solid foundation (budget) and cleaned out your debt (basement), you're ready to build the first pillar of your financial house - your emergency fund. Ensure you've done *both* before starting on your emergency fund. Why is that, you quizzically ask? Well, let's find out why. First of all, building a 6-month emergency fund is piggy principle #4.

1. Grow your income
2. Follow a written budget
3. Live debt free
4. **Build a 6-month emergency fund**
5. Save 10% of income for retirement
6. Pay it forward

When it comes to pay prioritization, you'll build your emergency fund *after* paying off your debt, but *before* you start saving for retirement. Do not try to accomplish two or three of these all at once. Remember, financial focus!

Reference your pay priority below.

Pay **Last** -->   #7 - Disposable (play money)
                    #6 - College Fund (if applicable)
                    #5 - Mortgage (if applicable)
                    #4 - Retirement (10% of take-home pay)
                    #3 - Emergency Fund (6-months of expenses)
                    #2 - Debt (100% debt-free, except house)
Pay **First** -->   #1 - Essential Living Expenses

Do you remember your budget's 6 superpowers? One of those superpowers is to help *build your emergency fund*. Without a budget, you have nothing to base your numbers on. As you'll soon learn, your budget is critical to calculating the amount required in your emergency fund. So, now you see why your budget is so important, let's see why being debt free is important as well.

Saving money towards an emergency fund while you still have debt is illogical. It's like drying yourself off with a towel while standing in the shower with the water on. Suppose you saved a $15,000 emergency fund, but still owe $15,000 in credit card debt; in reality, you have $0, no money at all! Being debt free allows you to powerfully build your emergency fund. Since your budget is complete and you're debt free, let's start by learning what an emergency fund is.

Simply put, an emergency fund exists to *prevent* debt; it's your cash cushion against all of life's surprises. It may help to think of it as a safety net for the flying trapeze artist. Can he fly without a net? Sure, if he loves living life on the edge! Me, I prefer a little safer approach - this is where your emergency fund comes in. Ok, so how the heck do we make one?

An emergency fund is built almost like you'd build a savings account. But first, we need to calculate how big it should be. A rich little piggy's emergency fund is equal to **6-months of essential living expenses**. In order to determine what that amount is, simply look at all of the expenses below the Crisis Line on your budget worksheet. Add all of those items up for a monthly total. In fact, if you've done your budget properly, they should already be totaled up, in the row "essential living total". You can see that in Phil's budget. Next, multiply that total by six; that's how much money you should have in your emergency fund. Wow, that budget sure does make things easy!

Why six months? Good question - there are many financial experts that will disagree, arm wrestle and sword fight over exactly how large your emergency fund should be. Some, daringly enough, will even question whether you should have one at all. However, most planners will advise having somewhere between 3-8 months of living expenses in your emergency fund. Piggy philosophy says **6 months** because in most cases that's long enough for you to find another income source should you lose your entire household income. Why not 2 or 3 months? Well, are we building a house of straw or a house of brick? How many people were unemployed for a *year* or more during the most recent great recession? Need I say more? Ok, so why not go 12 months or more? Well, simply put, that amount of money could be put to better use in other ways (retirement, mortgage, etc), rather than collecting dust in an emergency fund. Remember, it's six months of **essential living expenses** only; not your entire monthly budget. We'll see an example shortly. Your budget will also show you precisely how much extra income you can devote towards building your emergency fund. Until you have a full emergency fund in place, *extra* income is anything above your Crisis Line on your budget worksheet. You do not save for retirement, college, weddings, houses, or anything else that is not an *essential living expense* until your emergency fund is complete. This may seem a little harsh and this is where many simply give up. Don't! This is the peak of Mount Everest. On the other side, it's all downhill. The temporary struggle may be tough, but it will pay off with a lifetime of financial freedom. To have zero debt and a 6-month emergency fund is simply breathtaking. You'll feel like a million dollars!

You should only stop saving towards your emergency fund under two conditions. The *first*, is when you're complete; when you've saved six months of living expenses. The *second*, is if you have an actual emergency, in which case you put your savings on hold until the emergency is resolved, and then resume saving again. Once you've built a full emergency fund, there are some rules to follow.

Rule # 1 - Secure.

Emergency funds should be safe and sound. This means they should not be in volatile assets that can quickly drop in value; individual stocks, risky mutual funds, etc. The money belongs in a federally insured banking institution, in a simple savings or checking account. You will not earn much interest on this money, but the risk of losing it is even greater. Note: federally insured institution means member, FDIC (Federal Deposit Insurance Corporation) or NCUA (National Credit Union Association). Most banks are insured, but ask your bank if you're unsure. You can also use FDIC Bank Find or NCUA sites to find an insured bank. There are links in Appendix C.

Rule #2 - Liquid.

Funds should be easy to access. Ideally, within 24 hours. If the money is tied up in real estate or a 12-month certificate of deposit, it may take a while to get it out. Money that's sitting in a savings, checking, or money market account can be accessed by writing a check, using an ATM, or swiping your debit card. Even on weekends when the bank is closed, your money is still accessible. Remember, it's to handle an emergency!

Rule #3 - Emergencies only!

An emergency fund is to be used for exactly that - an emergency! What constitutes an emergency? If you've gotten this far (made a budget, you're debt free, and have an emergency fund), you're probably managing your finances properly enough that you won't have many emergencies. Hats off to you! By the way, it seems like the better your finances are, the less emergencies you tend to have. It's amazing how that works! However, just for fun, here are a few situations to ponder. Is it an emergency (Yes, No, Maybe)?

- Having a baby - NO. You have 9 months to budget.
- Large (unforeseen) medical bill - YES. Negotiate it down, pay in cash & replenish your emergency fund. Re-examine your healthcare coverage.
- Car repair - MAYBE. It depends on how much the repairs are. This is NOT an excuse to buy a brand new $25,000 vehicle.
- A single bread winner loses their job - YES. Your new job is now finding a new job. Start looking 12 hours a day, 7 days a week.
- Surprise tax bill - MAYBE. It depends on how much. Pay the IRS immediately. Adjust your tax withholdings to avoid a repeat next year, or budget for it.
- Wedding - NO. There's no rush; budget for it.

Remember, in the event you must "break glass" and dip into your emergency fund, that means all spending above the Crisis Line on your budget stops until your emergency fund is back at six months again. Yes, they do happen, but with proper planning, financial emergencies should be rare. Your emergency fund is not a savings account to be used for birthday presents, vacations, or new clothes. Discipline my little piggy - your financial house of brick depends upon it.

In fact, having an emergency fund is the most critical financial step you can take to avoid falling into debt.

There's one final thing to keep in mind about your emergency fund. Some people will say you don't need one and you can just use your credit card for emergencies. Or they'll say you can cash out some mutual funds for an emergency, allowing the money to possibly grow while not needed. Wrong. Piggy philosophy is fairly simple. As already stated, keep 6-months of living expenses in a federally insured financial institution (savings, checking, money market, etc) and follow the emergency fund rules above. Don't sabotage YOUR financial brick house with OTHER people's fancy tricks, gimmicks, or tight-rope walking antics. Remember whose door they'll be knocking on when the wind blows their straw house apart. Now that you're an emergency fund expert, let's apply one to Phil's situation.

Financial Status:

Financial Component	Status
Income	**Started; Growing**
Budget	**Complete**
Debt	**$0 (debt free)**
Emergency Fund	**Started; in progress**
Retirement	Chapter 7
House	Chapter 8
Estate Plan	Chapter 9
Insurance	Chapter 10
College Fund	Chapter 11

Phil's budget (after becoming DEBT FREE). He still earns $200/mo extra at a part-time job.

Monthly Pay (take-home)	Jun	Jul	Aug
Job =	$3,360		
Spouse's Job (N/A) =	$0		
Extra Job/Overtime (N/A) =	$200		
Total Income =	$3,560	$0	$0
Monthly Expenses	Jun	Jul	Aug
Entertainment	$0		
Eating Out	$0		
Miscellaneous	$0		
Cable TV	$0		
Cell Phone	$0		
Retirement	$0		
Emergency Fund	**$1,575**		
Discretionary Total =	$1,575	$0	$0
Gasoline (avg)	$210		
Car Maintenance (avg $420/yr)	$35		
Car Insurance	$80		
Renter's Insurance	$50		
Rent	$600		
Dental Insurance	$125		
Health Insurance	$250		
Electric (avg)	$160		
Water (avg)	$55		
Gas (avg)	$70		
Groceries (avg)	$350		
Essential Living Total =	$1,985	$0	$0
TOTAL Expenses =	$3,560	$0	$0
Excess =	$0	$0	$0

Budget Breakdown:

- Total Income = $3,560.
- Discretionary Total = $0; it all goes to emergency fund.
- Essential Living Total = $1,985.
- Total Expenses = $3,560.
- Excess = $1,575; it all goes to emergency fund.
- Debt = $0.
- Emergency Fund = requires $11,910 ($1,985 x 6).
- Retirement = $0 (resolve in Chapter 7).
- House = Renting (he buys a house in Chapter 8).
- Estate Plan = None (resolve in Chapter 9).
- Insurance = car, rent, dental, health (more in Chapter 10).
- College Fund = No kids (he has one in Chapter 11).

Notice Phil's emergency fund is based upon his essential living expenses of $1,985 per month. Since he has done a fairly good job of maintaining a written budget, it takes him no time at all to calculate his emergency fund. He simply multiplies the total by six (for six months). You can also see the benefit of minimizing your living expenses. The lower they are, the smaller the emergency fund you'll require. Additionally, you'll have more play money down the road.

Phil is *temporarily* living on a very tight budget in order to live like a Rich Little Pig for the *rest of his life*! He is focusing his financial efforts. In his case, for a bit longer than 7 months, he'll find enjoyment and pleasure without spending money on frivolities; cable TV, smart phones, eating out, movies, etc. He'll spend time with family and friends, play board games, workout, run, volunteer, go fishing, and do many other pleasurable things in life that don't require spending. In less than a year's time, Phil will have ample play money. When he's finished building his emergency fund, it'll be time to save for retirement.

[Pssst! If you're not quite as passionate as Phil, you'll be forgiven if you slow up a bit after building a 3-month emergency fund. It'll take a little longer to reach your full 6-months, but keep at it; you don't save for retirement until it's complete!]

KEY TAKEAWAYS
- Build your emergency fund *after* you:
    - Create your budget.
    - Become debt free.
- It should equal 6-months of essential living expenses.
- It must be secure, liquid, and for emergencies only!

"You can have excuses or results, not both." -Author Unknown

David W. Robbins

CHAPTER 7
RETIREMENT (PILLAR)

Retire early or retire late, it's up to you. Most people set out to retire based upon when they're eligible to receive Social Security payments. I say to heck with that; live like a rich little piggy and retire when you feel like it. Saving 10% for retirement is piggy principle #5.

1. Grow your income
2. Follow a written budget
3. Live debt free
4. Build a 6-month emergency fund
5. **Save 10% of income for retirement**
6. Pay it forward

When will you retire? How old will you be? How much monthly income will you need? How will you earn it? Sadly, if you ask people when they plan to retire, most will say they don't know, they haven't thought about it. Ask them where their income will come from when they retire and they don't know, they haven't thought about that either. Some will answer "Social Security". Some just shrug their shoulders, while others may laugh (or cry) and reply that they'll never be able to retire. What if tragedy strikes tomorrow, leaving you physically or mentally unable to work? These are questions that must be asked, and answered, if you plan to build a financial house of brick. You have the opportunity to live a comfortable, enjoyable and dignified retirement. You can choose when to retire and how much money you want in your retirement account. So, those are some typical questions most people think of when discussing retirement (how old, how much, etc). However, don't put the cart before the horse! Stick to the blueprint.

There's a method to the madness when it comes to planning your retirement. It's not an extremely complicated, burdensome process, but rather a relatively simple (2-step) piggy process. In order to understand how much money you'll need, you must *first* define what retirement means to you. *Secondly*, just as you did while planning your career goals, you apply a long-term strategy for achieving your retirement dreams. So, we begin by defining those dreams.

What is Retirement?

Retirement has a different meaning for everyone. *How would you define your retirement*? Maybe you want to continue working, but wish to work fewer hours. You may possibly want to travel the country or even the world. How about spending more time with family and friends? Do you enjoy any hobbies such as woodworking, pottery, hunting, fishing, or painting? Perhaps you'd like to pay some of your success forward by performing volunteer work in your community. Hey, the sky's the limit! The beauty is that *you* get to decide the terms of your retirement. Whatever you decide will be used to guide the cost of your expected standard of living. That, in turn, will be used to project how much money you'll need every month; your projected living expenses. Does this mean that once you paint a picture of what your retirement will be, that it can never change? Absolutely not. Does this mean that you're now locked in to doing exactly what you said you would when you retire? Absolutely not. It does mean, however, that you're now able to apply a *long-term retirement strategy* to help you achieve your retirement.

Long-Term Strategy

A *long-term retirement strategy* allows you to develop short and mid-term goals that will help you achieve your dreams. A short-term goal normally takes a few months and might involve paying off a credit card so you can save a few extra dollars towards retirement every month. A mid-term goal may take a few years to complete, such as completing a college degree. Each of your goals should, in some way, contribute towards your long-term retirement strategy. If not, reconsider having it as a goal. For example, buying a brand new $40,000 vehicle may sound nice, but how does that help your chances of retirement? For some people, figuring out this retirement thing can be tricky. The beauty is, you have sound piggy principles and a fantastic blueprint to follow in order to meet those goals. This just keeps getting better and better - life is good! Ok, we must start somewhere, so let's start by narrowing our focus.

There are many sources of income that can be used to fund, or partially fund, your retirement years besides a retirement account. Other sources of income include rental properties, business royalties, pensions, investments, stock dividends, bonds, and more. However, in keeping with the piggy philosophy, we're keeping things *simple* and focusing solely on **retirement accounts**. So, before going much further, let's find out what a retirement account is.

Retirement Account - What Is That?

You can think of a retirement account as a long-term investment account where you save your money for retirement. However, to explain a little further, understand that many types of investments can be deemed a "retirement account". For example, you are allowed to put a savings account, a certificate of deposit, stocks, and many other assets into a "retirement account". So, when you open one, either with your employer or your financial institution, be sure to ask for your investment options. *It is the tax benefit you receive that differentiates it from a "non-retirement" account.* We will not discuss detailed tax rules here because they are too complex and are better addressed by a certified tax professional. Many books are available on taxes and how to game, uh, I mean outsmart the system. Feel free to read them at your leisure, especially if you're having a hard time sleeping. There are many different types of retirement accounts, each with their own advantages and disadvantages. However, it is important to know the basic types. Search out the one that best suits your needs, depending on your current employment circumstances and retirement strategy. Here are the most common ones:

Individual Retirement Account (IRA).

This is arguably the one that most people think of when they hear the term 'retirement account'. In a nutshell, you generally put money into a traditional IRA *before* taxes. The money grows *tax-deferred* until you take it out in retirement. When you withdraw the money in retirement, you are then taxed at your applicable tax rate. If you take it out *early*, that is before minimum retirement age, you'll be subject to heavy taxes and penalties. Ask your financial institution about an IRA.

Roth IRA.

The Roth IRA has not been around as long as the traditional IRA, but is quite common. Unlike an IRA, when investing in a Roth IRA, you do so *after* taxes. You pay taxes on your earnings *first* and then put it into your Roth IRA. The money grows *tax-free*, with *tax-free* withdrawals in retirement, provided you meet specific conditions. Ask your financial institution about a Roth IRA.

401(K).

The 401(K) gets its name from the section of tax code

that governs it. These are offered or sponsored by an employer. If your employer offers a 401(K) retirement program, you can contribute to your retirement account *before* taxes. Like a traditional IRA, the money grows *tax-deferred* until you take it out in retirement. When you withdraw the money in retirement, you are then taxed at your applicable tax rate. If you take it *early*, that is before minimum retirement age, you'll be subject to heavy taxes and penalties. Some employers offer matching contributions to your 401(K) - this is like *free* money! If you leave your employer, you should research IRA rollover options to take your money with you.

Thrift Savings Plan (TSP).

The TSP is a retirement savings and investment plan for federal employees, including military members. They offer traditional IRA (tax-deferred) and Roth IRA (tax-free) investment plans. Some agencies will offer matching contributions - yes, more *free* money! If you're considering employment with the federal government, be sure to ask about the TSP.

403(b).

Like the 401(K), the 403(b) gets its name from the section of tax code that governs it. The 403b is a retirement plan offered by certain public schools and tax-exempt/non-profit organizations. Like the 401(K), contributions are made *before* taxes and grow *tax-deferred*. Ask your employer about a 403(b).

When it comes to retirement accounts, you'll often hear much debate about whether the IRA or the Roth IRA is "better". Well, again, it comes down to simple math. This is more complex than is required for our purposes, but below are the general pros and cons of each, to help you get an idea. You can research the many other differences between the two online. There are also online calculators that let you enter variables to compare the two, but don't over think yourself. Without the headache math, my personal choice is the Roth IRA because I like knowing my money will be tax-free during retirement. However, having either is far better than having none - do not delay!

IRA.

Pro: If you earn $100 and put it into your IRA, you'll have $100 in your IRA. It goes into your IRA *before* any taxes. That allows 100% of your money to grow.

Con: IRA money grows *tax-deferred*. That means you'll pay taxes on it when you pull it out in retirement. What will your tax rate be during retirement?

Roth IRA.

Pro: Roth IRA money grows *tax-free*. That means you'll pay no taxes on it when you pull it out in retirement.

Con: If you earn $100 and put it into your Roth IRA, you will have *about* $75 in your Roth IRA. That's because it goes into your Roth IRA *after* taxes; so what is your tax rate? That allows 75% of your money to grow (more/less, depending on your tax rate).

Regardless of which you choose, each retirement account that you're eligible for should be thoroughly researched before deciding on which one to use. There are different contribution limits, vesting periods, tax consequences and many other considerations that can affect your retirement strategy. Take some time to discuss this decision with your tax professional or financial planner. However, the bottom line is to invest! Do your research, pick one and start contributing! Which is better? Put it this way - one is better than none! In some instances, you may have TWO retirement accounts. For example, if your employer offers a 401(K), you can also open a traditional IRA or Roth IRA through your financial institution. Ok, so once you decide on a retirement account, you want to know *when* and *how* to save.

When to Save for Retirement

Piggy principle #5 is to save 10% of income for retirement. You do this by *first* creating your budget, *then* becoming debt free, and *finally*, building your 6-month emergency fund. Once all three of those steps are complete, you'll be ready to start investing for retirement! Why not just start saving right away? Good question; it's important to know why we're building our financial house this way, so let's explain a bit further. Refer to our piggy pay priority below for reference and notice where retirement falls.

Rich Little Piggy

Pay **Last** -->   #7 - Disposable (play money)
                #6 - College Fund (if applicable)
                #5 - Mortgage (if applicable)
                #4 - Retirement (10% of take-home pay)
                #3 - Emergency Fund (6-months of expenses)
                #2 - Debt (100% debt-free, except house)
Pay **First** -->   #1 - Essential Living Expenses

Right _here_ is where too many people flush away their retirement and end up living on food stamps and payday loans in their golden years. Right _here_ is where people choose lattes, eating out, smart phones, high-def cable packages and many other "luxuries" in life over a stable, sound, dignified retirement. If you can afford those things, great, but your retirement comes **_first_**. Remember your piggy philosophy. Furthermore, remember that you're always growing your income, so maybe you can "only" afford 1 latte a week right now (or maybe none) after funding your retirement account, but later, you'll be able to afford as many as you want, and without sacrificing your future. Right now, I want you to press the "test" button on your smoke alarm and tape it down so the alarm does not stop screeching until you have set up automatic monthly deposits into your retirement account! No, not really, but that's the mindset you need to have. Start saving for retirement today.

Now, what if you pay all of your essential living expenses and there's no money left to save for retirement? That's called having too much month left at the end of the money! In that case, you'll have to do what's necessary to lower your living expenses by cutting back here and there. At some point, when it's down to bare bones, you're left with one last alternative; Piggy Principle #1 - Grow Your Income. You should be growing your income anyway, but this may be time to hit the little red 'turbo-boost' button! Either you're living too large (expenses too high), and/or you need more income. Maybe take on a roommate temporarily. Maybe move to a cheaper house. There are options to consider.

You would not start building the walls of your house before laying the foundation (*budget*). In the same regard, you can not properly plan for retirement without building a budget. Remember, one of the superpowers of your budget is to *enable you to fund your retirement*. Just as it helped build your emergency fund, your budget will also help fund your retirement. You won't even know if you have free money to save without first consulting your budget. So, not only is having a budget critical before saving for retirement, but so is being debt free.

Becoming *debt free* is paramount before starting to save for retirement. It will provide you with the financial clean slate necessary to start saving. For example, if you had $250 of discretionary income that you wanted to save for retirement, but you still owed $10,000 on your credit card, in reality you don't have $250 of discretionary income. In fact, you have NO discretionary income at all until you pay off your debt! That $10,000 is not yours, it's the banks. Have you ever loaned money to someone and they have a hard time paying you back? But when you see that person around town, they're buying a new smart phone or eating out at a fancy restaurant. You may think to yourself "hmmm, they have money to spend on that, but yet they don't have money to pay me back?!" Funny how that works. So, getting debt free brings you to the last step required before starting to save.

The last step required to complete before you start saving for retirement is to build your 6-month *emergency fund*. Failing to do so will inevitably result in falling right back into debt again! You must have a cushion to protect yourself from life's little surprises. That way, you can save for retirement stress free. So, now you understand *why* you save for retirement only after creating a budget, becoming debt free and building your emergency fund. Now, you need to know *how* to start saving.

How to Save for Retirement

Piggy Principle #5 says to save 10% of income for retirement. Why 10%? Why take-home (net) pay and not before tax (gross) pay? It's not some magical number by any means. To be perfectly blunt, it's a starting point! Many experts will advise you to save 10-15% of your income for retirement. Some will say it's *before* tax savings, while others will say it's *after* tax savings. Piggy philosophy is simple and geared towards working class folks like myself. Psychologically, many folks see 15% as insurmountable and unrealistic, so they throw up their hands and don't save anything. Ouch! So, by easing in to something within arms' reach...something realistic, the idea is to start saving at least *something* and build on your success. Oh, and becoming a millionaire in the process doesn't hurt either. Many factors affect how much you should save, and you must factor these in when planning your retirement. Just some of these factors are as follows.

- How long you'll save (retirement age minus current age).
- Average return on your investment (4%, 8%, 12%, etc).
- How much income you'll require in retirement.
- Your income while you're saving ($30K, $50K, $100K)?
- Tax implications (tax-free, tax-deferred, tax bracket, etc).
- Will you have Social Security and if so, how much?
- Will you have a pension and if so, how much?

As you can see, there's a lot to consider. However, you must start somewhere, so start! Piggy philosophy is to save 10% of your take-home pay, but depending on your circumstances, more may be required. The nice thing is that math always works! If you do the math and you won't have enough on 10%, then save more; it's that simple. It may not be *easy* to save 15% or more, depending on how late you start in life, but the math is simple. You can't argue with math; it is what it is.

Figuring out *how* to save 10% of your income for retirement can be a daunting task, if you let it - don't. This book is not about investing, so investment advice on specific stocks, funds, and bonds will not be given here. It is, however, about building a solid financial house and therefore, you must have basic knowledge of how to save for your retirement. My advice is to start with the person or office that administers your retirement plan. For example, if your employer offers a 401(K), speak with the human resources office for options and explanations of their investments. Same for the TSP; ask your agency for assistance and information on their investment options. You can also consult a financial planner regarding IRAs, but if you do so, ensure they do not receive any commissions or fees for their recommendations. You want a fee-based planner; one that advises and teaches how to invest and gets paid a small, flat fee, whether or not you invest in *their* particular products. It's also easy enough to start online with a reputable investment company. I don't recommend any certain ones, but Vanguard and Fidelity are just two examples. There are additional links in Appendix C, so shop around. You should compare fees and expenses among your investment options. Regardless of what you choose to invest in, the basic function of *how* will remain the same. Piggy philosophy is to save 10% of your take-home pay. Employer matching contributions *DO* count towards that 10%! Let's walk through an example of *how* this would happen.

Hypothetical Financial Status:

- **Your Salary**: $52,800 (before tax).
- **Take-Home Pay**: $3,300/month. (approximate; after taxes, exemptions, SSA, Medicare)
- **Save 10% for Retirement:** $330/month ($3,300 x .10).
- **Retirement Account:** Employer-sponsored 401(K).
- **Matching Contributions:** Yes, they offer matching contributions, up to 5% of your salary.

Retirement Action Plan:

- You save 5% of your salary ($52,800 x .05) = $2,640/yr ($220/month); this comes out *pre-tax*.
- Your 5% employer match is $2,640/yr ($220/month); this is *free* money!
- Total savings to your 401(K) = $5,280/yr ($440/month); *more* than $330/mo (10% of take-home).
- Your new take-home pay is $3,080/mo* (original $3,300 - $220 in retirement savings).
* Your take-home pay will actually be a bit higher because the $220 is *pre-tax* money.

Retirement Results:

So, for $220/mo (plus employer match), you'll have about $1.5 Million in retirement!*
* Assumes employer match ($220/mo), 8% return after fees/expenses, compounded monthly.
* Average S&P 500 return (1973-2013) was about 12% - you'd have around **$4.5 Million!**

Piggy Point to Ponder:

The employer match is powerful. In this example, you need to save $330/month for retirement. You saved $220 pre-tax and your employer match is $220, for a total of $440. That $440 is *more* than 10% of your take-home pay. So, for $220 (not $330), you've exceeded your retirement savings goal. If your employer offers matching contributions, always, always contribute up to the match - it's FREE money!

[Personal Note: I received a 5% TSP match as a federal employee. It was great!]

The above example is nice because the employer provided a 5% match. However, if they did not, then you'd simply save the original $330 per month, leaving your new take-home pay at approximately $2,970 ($3,300 - $330). It would actually be a bit higher because it would be *pre-tax* money; remember, you only receive about 70-75% of every dollar you earn after taxes and deductions. Even at $330/mo, under the same 8% investment scenario, you'd have about **$1.1 Million** in retirement! Not too shabby for a working-class piggy from the neighborhood.

What if you're able to save *more* than 10% towards retirement? Well, if you follow the Piggy Principles, you'll most certainly be able to invest far more towards retirement than 10% of your income. Feel free to invest more if you like, but ideally, there's no need to invest more than 15% max until if/when you've met other financial goals. For example, we'll discuss buying a house in Chapter 8. If you have, or plan to have children, you'll want to save for their college funds (Chapter 11). You'll also use your money to enjoy life and help others, in line with the Piggy Philosophy. As with any rule, there are exceptions and it's not possible to cover every single situation. As stated earlier, if you start late in life and don't have 40 years to invest, then you should target more than 10%, but always following the piggy principles. Just remember that once invested, your money stays invested.

As previously stated in Chapter 5, one of the four Debt Don'ts is to NEVER borrow from your retirement! It almost helps to think of retirement savings as a one-way process. Once the money is invested, it can never come out until retirement.

So, now that we've seen how and when to save for retirement, let's look at our buddy Phil and see how his retirement savings is coming along.

Financial Status:

Financial Component	Status
Income	**Started; Growing**
Budget	**Complete**
Debt	**$0 (debt free)**
Emergency Fund	**Complete**
Retirement	**Started; saving 10% of income**
House	Chapter 8
Estate Plan	Chapter 9
Insurance	Chapter 10
College Fund	Chapter 11

Phil's current budget looks something like the following. You'll notice he quit his part-time job and is no longer earning an extra $200 per month.

Updates in gray and **bold**.

Monthly Pay (take-home)	Jun	Jul	Aug
Job =	$3,360		
Spouse's Job (N/A) =	$0		
Extra Job/Overtime (N/A) =	**$0**		
Total Income =	**$3,360**	$0	$0
Monthly Expenses	Jun	Jul	Aug
Entertainment	**$200**		
Eating Out	**$125**		
Miscellaneous	**$45**		
Cable TV	**$85**		
Cell Phone	**$45**		
Retirement	**$336**		
Discretionary Total =	**$836**	$0	$0
Gasoline (avg)	$210		
Car Maintenance (avg $420/yr)	$35		
Car Insurance	$80		
Renter's Insurance	$50		
Rent	$600		
Dental Insurance	$125		
Health Insurance	$250		
Electric (avg)	$160		
Water (avg)	$55		
Gas (avg)	$70		
Groceries (avg)	$350		
Essential Living Total =	$1,985	$0	$0
TOTAL Expenses =	**$2,821**	$0	$0
Excess =	**$539**	$0	$0

Budget Breakdown:

- Total Income = $3,360.
- Discretionary Total = $836.
- Essential Living Total = $1,985.
- Total Expenses = $2,281.
- Excess = $539.
- Debt = $0.
- Emergency Fund = $11,910 ($1,985 x 6).
- Retirement = $336 (on track; 10% of take-home pay).
- House = Renting (he buys a house in Chapter 8).
- Estate Plan = None (resolve in Chapter 9).
- Insurance = car, rent, dental, health (more in Chapter 10).
- College Fund = No kids (he has one in Chapter 11).
- Emergency fund expense dropped off - it's fully funded.
- Discretionary spending resumed, but Phil's made wiser spending choices (entertainment, eating out, cable TV, cell phone); total monthly savings of $268.

Phil's Retirement Outlook:

We can see in Phil's biography that his retirement dream is to fly fish and travel to all 50 states. His long-term strategy is for his retirement income to be the same as his current income, without having to work. This would free up his time to allow for fishing and traveling. How does he achieve his strategy? Phil adheres to Piggy Principle #5 - Save 10% of income for retirement. Why does he choose 10% and not more? Well, as stated, Phil ran the math and 10% will allow him to meet his retirement goals. He arrived at that number as follows.

- Desired retirement income: the same as it is now, $3,360/mo ($40,320/yr).
- If Phil can earn 4% interest on a $1 Million nest egg, it will return $3,333/mo ($40,000/yr).
- If he invests $336/mo for 40 years, at 8% interest, he'll have about $1.1 Million.
- $1.1 Million earning 4% interest generates $3,666/mo ($44,000/yr).
- Retirement outlook: awesome!

Note: he estimates 8% interest during his investing years but only 4% in retirement. This is because of risk/reward theory. Over a 40-year period, you can generally invest in growth and aggressive growth funds and ride out any down periods. However, in retirement you want much less risk, so you'd therefore shift your money to a lower risk investment fund, thereby incurring lower reward over the long term.

Keep in mind, this is a retirement *estimate* in a *hypothetical* example, using Phil's budget. It's impossible to forecast an *exact* retirement plan 40 years out under every possible scenario, but you must start somewhere. Start somewhere or go nowhere, it's up to you. Here are some "Best-Case / Worst-Case" retirement assumptions that Phil should consider.

Best-Case Assumptions:
- Social Security will add even *more* to his income.
- He may average *more* than 8% over 40 years (S&P 500 has averaged around 12%).
- Income will go up over those 40 years (and percentage of

savings; much bigger nest egg).
- He may have (or get) a job that offers a pension; adds even *more* to income.
- He may have (or get) a job that offers a MATCH in retirement savings; *bigger* nest egg.
- He'll own a house by retirement, dropping $600 of his current living expenses.
- His retirement account could be tax-free in retirement (i.e. Roth IRA).
- He starts sooner than age 25; *bigger* nest egg.

Worst-Case Assumptions:
- Possibly *little* or *no* Social Security will be available (depleted/bankrupt).
- He may average *less* than 8% over 40 years (or lose his *entire* investment).
- Income will go *down* over those 40 years (will not be able to meet retirement goal).
- His retirement account could be taxable in retirement (i.e. Traditional IRA).
- Retirement account fees/expenses reduce his growth.
- He starts later than age 25; *smaller* nest egg.

Looking over these assumptions, you can clearly see why **income** (Chapter 2) is so important to retirement; it is the front-end of the process. Always grow your income, thereby increasing retirement savings. Also consider a job that offers a pension and a retirement account, ideally with matching contributions. Even a relatively modest pension can have a significant impact on your retirement years. For example, if you had $300,000 in your retirement account at age 65, it would earn $12,000 per year at a 4 percent interest rate ($1,000/month). So, if your company offered a pension of $1,000 per month, it would be the equivalent of having $300,000 in your retirement account earning 4 percent interest. That's not too shabby. You can see how it all works together. Unfortunately, too many financial experts focus primarily on the back-end of the process; compound interest calculators showing how much you'll have if you save so much money per month. As you can see, there's a lot more to it than that. That's why the Piggy Philosophy takes a holistic view of financial success. Keep it simple; work and save, save and work. How likely do you think each of these best and worst-case assumptions are? There are many assumptions to consider, but let's look a little closer at one in particular.

One major retirement assumption for most people is determining what amount of Social Security, if any, will be available when they retire. I would not advise relying on Social Security, but if you're within 10-20 years of retirement, it doesn't hurt to at least be aware of what you may receive. In order to get an idea of what your payments might be, you can use the retirement estimator on the Social Security Administration's website (see Appendix C). It's relatively easy to use and will give you an estimated monthly benefit, based upon what you've already paid in and your current projected earnings. Simply enter your name, social security number, birth date, and some other basic information and it will provide you with estimates on early, full, and late retirement benefits. The longer you wait to claim your benefits, the higher your monthly benefits will be. For example, claiming at age 62 might pay $800 per month, whereas waiting until 67 might pay $1,200 per month. As their site states, keep in mind it's only an estimate. For what it's worth, according to the Social Security Administration, the average retired worker's monthly benefit is $1,294 (from December 2013 data). Wow, even *double* that amount would be pretty tough to live on. That's why it's so important to build your retirement account and consider a job that offers a pension. So, once your retirement savings is in motion, it may be time to set your sights on a house.

Key Takeaways:

- Start saving for retirement *after* you:
    - Create your budget.
    - Become debt free.
    - Build a 6-month emergency fund.
- Follow a long-term strategy to reach your retirement goals.
- Save 10% of your income for retirement (more if needed).
- NEVER borrow from your retirement.

"It's not about how much money you *make*, but how much you *save*." -Author Unknown

David W. Robbins

CHAPTER 8
HOUSE (PILLAR)

Ahhh...baked apple pie, a white picket fence, fresh cut grass, a tire swing hanging in the backyard...the dreamy visions of home ownership. Or wait...is it roof repairs, a broken AC unit, plumbing problems, water damage, termites, stressful mortgage payments and a foreclosure sign?! More so a Nightmare on Elm Street? Owning a house can be a delight or a disaster! It can be a warm, loving place where you raise your family and grow old in your golden years, or it can be an anchor around your neck that causes headaches and chest pains. Once you sign on the dotted line, you're no longer dedicated to purchasing a home, you're *committed*. What's the difference between dedicated and committed, you ask? Well, if you enjoyed a nice breakfast of bacon and eggs this morning, remember the two parties that helped make it happen. The first is the chicken...the chicken was *dedicated* to your breakfast. However, the pig...the pig was *committed*! <cue the

laughter> Ok, enough lame jokes. Being committed to home ownership should come at the proper time in your life and with careful consideration of your financial matters.

When to Buy a House?

Piggy philosophy says you should buy a house only after you've created a budget, paid off all debt, built your emergency fund, and have started saving 10% of income towards retirement. Refer to the pay priority below. I think the *why* of this should now be coming clear. A budget, if used properly, has a superpower that enables you to afford your house. Being debt free allows you to powerfully build your emergency fund. Your emergency fund shields you from many of life's surprises and not having one is a **major** reason why people fall into debt. Just because you've done all this does not mean you must run out and buy a house. Think back to your career and retirement strategies.

Pay **Last** --> #7 - Disposable (play money)
　　　　　　　#6 - College Fund (if applicable)
　　　　　　　#5 - Mortgage (if applicable)
　　　　　　　#4 - Retirement (10% of take-home pay)
　　　　　　　#3 - Emergency Fund (6-months of expenses)
　　　　　　　#2 - Debt (100% debt-free, except house)
Pay **First** --> #1 - Essential Living Expenses

You career and retirement long-term strategies can impact when you should buy a house. For example, call me crazy, but notice that buying a house is not included in the Piggy Principles. Did that get overlooked by mistake? Was it a printing error? No, it was neither. Piggy Principles are things you should *always* do. The reality is that today's workforce is far more mobile than it was a few decades ago. Some people will choose to pursue their careers rather than own a home, which is perfectly fine. In fact, I'd argue that *should* be the case, at least during the early years of your career. Remember that thing called 'mobility'; use it to boost your career earnings. You can also have your cake and eat it too. By delaying the purchase of a new home, you can grow your income exponentially, rent inexpensively, and bank lots of money. Then, later in life, when the time is right, you pay *cash* for your house or, at the least, have a very large down payment.

Additionally, some people may have a dream to move around in retirement and enjoy the freedom that renting offers. They may live "here and there" for a few years at a time, enjoying the sandy beaches of Florida, the majestic mountains of Colorado, the city life of New York, or even live overseas for a while. In that event, constantly buying and selling will be very costly. Buy a house, but buy it when you're ready! Build your *financial* house before your *dream* house. However, for the many who are ready to own a home, there are a few financial matters to consider.

What to Consider When Buying a House.

There are many things to consider when purchasing a house. A lot of people get in a rush to own a house because they think they're wasting money on rent. Just remember there's a big difference between *owning* a home and *owing* on a home. When buying a house, there are 3 very important rules to follow in order to live in a financial house of brick.

House Rule #1 - Down Payment.

You must save up enough money to put at least 20% down on your house. For example, if the house will cost $150,000, your down payment should be at least $30,000. This does not mean you stop saving for retirement in order to do so. Neither does this mean using your emergency fund towards your down payment; buying a house is not an emergency. If you put down anything less than 20%, the lender will most likely require you to pay private mortgage insurance (PMI). PMI protects the lender if you default on your loan. Additionally, who remembers that little thing called the "housing bubble", starting around 2006-2007? People to this day are *still* underwater in their homes; they owe more than it's worth. For many, if they had put more money down, they might be at least at break-even by now. If you can't afford 20% down, you really can't afford the house. It means you're not financially ready to make a purchase of this magnitude. It's true, in some cases you can buy a house with no, or a very small down payment.

People who qualify for a Veterans Administration loan can often obtain a loan with no down payment or PMI. Some mortgage companies are also known to get "creative" with lending terms (minimal down, interest-only, etc). There are also special government programs that exist to assist under-privileged and/or under-served communities that historically, have had low ownership rates. However, if you're unable to put 20% down, you should re-assess your endeavor to purchase a home for the time being. Having a 20% down payment is just one rule to follow.

House Rule #2 - Monthly Payments.

Once you've saved at least a 20% down payment, you must examine your budget to ensure your house payment is no more than 25% of your take-home pay. For example, if your take-home pay is $3,800 per month, your mortgage should be no more than $950 per month, including principal and interest. Realize, you must also budget separately for taxes, insurance, and maintenance. If a house costs $150,000, you must put at least $30,000 down. Then, you get a 15-year mortgage on the remaining $120,000 at a 4% fixed interest rate. Your monthly payment will be $887 per month; well under 25% of your income.

House Rule #3 - Mortgage Terms.

When taking out a loan on a house, always get a 15-year mortgage with a *fixed* interest rate. Getting a longer mortgage (i.e. 30 years) will give you lower monthly payments, but it will also take you 15 years longer to pay off and cost a lot more in interest. Taking out a 30-year mortgage is similar to taking out a 5, 6, or 7-year car loan; it's not financially smart. By trying to extend the payments out, you're trying to afford something that you really can't. Inevitably, disaster will strike and you'll be back to digging out of debt. Don't do it. The same holds true for adjustable rate mortgages that seem nice when the rate is lower than a fixed rate, at least initially. However, when the economy shifts and the Federal Reserve starts raising rates, you can find yourself quickly drowning in house payments. The streets are littered with foreclosures of those who thought they'd be "smart" and take out an adjustable rate mortgage; don't be next.

Besides the major 3 house rules, there are some other factors to consider when buying a house. Just like most things, a house will eventually need maintenance and repairs. Pipes burst, roofs leak, appliances break, and walls need painting. Some items can be minor, while others can be quite costly (i.e. tens of thousands of dollars). Additionally, you must budget for property taxes and homeowners insurance. If your house is in a flood zone, you'll also require flood insurance, which can be quite expensive. More on insurance in Chapter 10. Some houses are located in a community that has a homeowners association (HOA). This may require additional expenses for monthly HOA dues and/or community development fees. These costs are to maintain common areas, such as lawn maintenance, landscaping, community pools, club house, and more. Be sure to research HOA restrictions very thoroughly *before* purchasing a home. Some associations will dictate what kind of fence you can have, how tall it can be, what colors you're allowed to paint your house, how often you can water your lawn, where you can park your car, and many other such factors. Since you asked, my advice is to never buy a home with an HOA.

At this stage of building your financial house of brick,

it's important to note that you should be financially stable. All of your budgeting and debt are taken care of, your emergency fund and retirement have been addressed, and you've decided to purchase the house of your dreams. Depending on how much discretionary income you have, it would be appropriate to pay extra payments on your house. For example, on our $120,000 loan above (15-year, 4% interest), we had a payment of $887 per month. When you include the interest, you will have paid about $160,000 on that $120,000 loan. However, by paying an extra $200 per month, you can save almost $10,000 in interest and pay off the mortgage more than 3 years early. How aggressive you get with this is up to you. That's one reason you really shouldn't rush to save more than 15% of your income towards retirement. Any extra money you have beyond 15% should be used to pay down your mortgage. The benefit of owning (not owing) your home can not be overstated.

By now, you can see the power of being debt free, so just imagine if your house was 100% paid off! Picture your budget worksheet with NO house payment on it. Suppose your mortgage payment is $1,000 per month. Just like we described with a pension of $1,000 per month, that's equivalent to having $300,000 in a retirement account earning 4 percent interest. So, by paying off your mortgage before you retire, it's like saving at least $300,000 in a retirement account. Nice! It's amazing the way this piggy blueprint helps everything fall right into place. A paid-off house can fit in nicely with your retirement years; it's up to you to make it happen. Speaking of making it happen, let's see how Phil is doing with *his* house.

So, Phil is doing well so far. He decided to settle down and buy a house. He found a squeal of a deal in a desirable neighborhood for only $135,000. It's not a mansion, but it's a small 3-bedroom starter home. He put down $27,000, which is 20 percent of the list price. He financed the remainder ($108,000) on a 15-year loan at a fixed 4 percent interest rate. His monthly payment is about $800 per month. As part of home ownership, Phil has also added property taxes and homeowners insurance to his budget. By living within his means, Phil has not only purchased a home, but he's also debt free and has a 6-month emergency fund. So, if he encounters any maintenance problems with his house, he can easily afford to get them fixed. No headaches, no loans, and no problems. You can see how much easier it is to buy a house when your financial affairs are in order.

Financial Status:

Financial Component	Status
Income	Started; Growing
Budget	Complete
Debt	$0 (debt free)
Emergency Fund	Complete
Retirement	Started; saving 10% of income
House	15-year, 4% fixed rate loan
Estate Plan	Chapter 9
Insurance	Chapter 10
College Fund	Chapter 11

Phil's budget worksheet. Updates in gray & **bold**.

Monthly Pay (take-home)	Jul	Aug	Sep
Job =	$3,360		
Spouse's Job (N/A) =	$0		
Extra Job/Overtime (N/A) =	$0		
Total Income =	$3,360	$0	$0

Monthly Expenses	Jun	Jul	Aug
Entertainment	$200		
Eating Out	$125		
Miscellaneous	$45		
Cable TV	$85		
Cell Phone	$45		
Retirement	$336		
Discretionary Total =	$836	$0	$0
Gasoline (avg)	$210		
Car Maintenance (avg $420/yr)	$35		
Car Insurance	$80		
Property Taxes	**$100**		
Homeowner's Insurance	**$90**		
Mortgage	**$800**		
Dental Insurance	$125		
Health Insurance	$250		
Electric (avg)	$160		
Water (avg)	$55		
Gas (avg)	$70		
Groceries (avg)	$350		
Essential Living Total =	**$2,325**	$0	$0
TOTAL Expenses =	**$3,161**	$0	$0
Excess =	**$199**	$0	$0

Budget Breakdown:

- Total Income = $3,360.
- Discretionary Total = $836.
- Essential Living Total = $2,325.
- Total Expenses = $3,161.
- Excess = $199.
- Debt = $0.
- Emergency Fund = $11,910 ($1,985 x 6).
- Retirement = $336 (on track; 10% of take-home pay).
- House = 15-yr, 4% fixed rate loan.
- Estate Plan = None (resolve in Chapter 9).
- Insurance = car, rent, dental, health (more in Chapter 10).
- College Fund = No kids (he has one in Chapter 11).

As Phil moves along in life, he's finally decided to settle down in a home of his own. Buying a house is a major milestone in life and also increases the value of your estate. Speaking of estates, if you haven't already, it's critical that you examine your estate plan.

Key Takeaways:

- Buy a house *after* you:
    - Create your budget.
    - Become debt free.
    - Build a 6-month emergency fund.
    - Start saving 10% of income for retirement
- House Rule #1 - Down Payment
    - Always put at least 20% down.
- House Rule #2 - Monthly Payments
    - Payments should be under 25% of take-home pay.
- House Rule #3 - Mortgage Terms
    - Take out a 15-year, fixed rate loan.

"The goal isn't more money. The goal is living life on your terms." -Chris Brogan

CHAPTER 9
ESTATE PLAN (PILLAR)

Phil: "Brother, if I die, I want you to have my gold watch."

Brother: "Well, if I die, I want you to have my motorcycle."

Hmm. See if you can figure out what's wrong with the above discussion. If you can't figure it out. the answer is "IF". Phil and his brother should be saying "When" I die, not "If" I die. Do you know what day YOU will die? How about what month? Ok, what YEAR will you die? Exactly - with rare exception, most of us do not know when we'll die. It could be tomorrow, next month, or next year, who knows. If you're like most people, you rarely think about dying in specific calendar terms.

Although many of us don't like to talk about death, guess what, 100% of us will die. You work hard to earn a living. You work hard to buy a house. You work hard to save money, slash debt and buy nice things. What happens to it all, not if, but WHEN you die? The easy response is to not care; who cares, I'll be dead anyway, right? That's true, but I would argue a fairly lazy and selfish thought on your behalf. Who will care for your children? Who will care for your ailing parents? Do you care about them? How about your pets? For the minority of people who don't have *any* family or loved ones in their lives, estate planning may be simplified to just themselves, or their preferred charity. So, to those "lone wolf" individuals without anybody in your life, you'd rather have the state get your money than a friend? Are you immune from illness and injury? Because who will speak on your behalf if you're unable to speak due to an accident or illness? Most people have at least *one* or more family members they'd like to receive their estate when they're gone, even if it's just a few hundred dollars. Do your heirs even know what assets you have? Will they know that you have a savings account at Bank ABC? Will they know that you have a mutual fund that you've been saving in for the last 15 years? Do they know your medical wishes should you be on life support? Maybe you prefer they shuffle through your entire house, looking and hoping to find everything when you die. Maybe it will go unclaimed because nobody knew it existed. Lots and lots of questions, but this is where estate planning fits in to our financial house of brick.

Everyone should have an estate plan. Not just old people, married people, rich people, or people with kids, but everyone. Some estate plans are simpler than others, but they all serve the same basic purpose; to designate what happens to you and your stuff when you're sick, injured or dead. Oh, but where to begin? Well, remember your trusty budget. One of your budget's superpowers enables you to *manage your estate plan.* It gives you a comprehensive view of your income, expenses, debt, retirement savings, and more. Use it as a baseline to determine how your income will be replaced and how your family will manage upon your death. Use it to determine what debt you may have and how it will be handled upon your death. Some debt dies with you, but some does not; don't burden your family due to a lack of planning. Let's take a look at some things to consider, but be advised you should always consult a qualified attorney or estate planning professional when preparing legal documents.

Pensions.

If you have a pension, what happens to it when you die? Well, it depends. If you're already receiving a pension, odds are good that you were advised to make a decision on survivor benefits. Generally speaking, if you take a slightly smaller pension, you can designate a beneficiary to receive all, or some, of your pension when you die. If you elect to take your full pension, then it almost always dies along with you; nobody gets it when you die. Sometimes this decision is irrevocable once you make your decision, while some pensions offer you a small window of opportunity to change your mind. For example, before you retire, your employer will ask you to decide if you want a full pension or a reduced pension with survivor benefits. Your full pension might be $1,800 per month, but with survivor benefits, it may be

$1,500 per month (or something similar). In return for giving up that $300 per month, your beneficiary would receive a portion of your pension in the event of your death. You'll have to make your decision in writing. In this example, your decision may be irreversible. However, it's possible you may have a 1-year window within which time you can change your mind. The details are not what matter here, but rather the knowledge and awareness to factor this decision into your financial affairs. Obviously, there is no "right" decision, but ask yourself how much term life insurance you could get with the difference. In the scenario just described, the difference is $300 per month between pensions with and without survivor benefits. So, how much term life insurance could you get on yourself for $300 per month? Would it be mathematically beneficial to your heirs to receive your remaining pension or a lump sum life insurance policy? Also consider tax implications; generally, life insurance proceeds are not taxable. So, if you have one, or will be receiving one, a pension is just one consideration in estate planning.

So, what about your stuff? Who gets all of your stuff when you die? What happens to you if you're in a coma or on life support? Who takes care of your kids? These questions are answered by legal estate planning documents. There are many legal documents used in estate planning, but we'll focus on the more common ones you should consider. Some are simpler than others, but most should be completed under advice of a qualified professional. If not, you run the risk of them being as useful as a rolled up newspaper. Depending on the laws, many of these documents, and their requirements are *state-specific*, so please bear that in mind. Some must be notarized, while others do not. Below are some common estate planning documents that you should discuss with your attorney or estate planner (not all-inclusive).

Will.

A Will is a written document that can do many things, but most know it for telling people what to do with their stuff (assets) when they die. You can also appoint an executor of your Will, name guardians for your children, provide for pets, and many other things.

Be advised, beneficiaries listed on financial accounts, insurance policies, and other assets normally take precedence over Wills. For example, if you leave "everything" to your child in your Will, but your ex-spouse from 7 years ago is still named as the beneficiary on your $500,000 life insurance policy, guess what? Yeah, that's why it's important to ensure your paperwork is up to date and if you have any questions, consult a qualified professional.

"My husband gets the jet skis when I die - he knows that."
"My sister knows she gets my house - I already told her."
"My kids get everything."

Yeah, that's what *you* think! It's amazing how well your wishes and words are remembered (or not) when you die. It's amazing how the state gets to make key decisions about YOUR stuff during probate because you did not take the time to get a Will done. Don't leave it to chance - document it. Get a Will!

Living Will.

A living Will is a legal document that states your preferences for medical care if you're unable to make decisions for yourself. They can also be known as an Advanced Medical Directive, Medical Power of Attorney, Personal Directive, or something similar, depending on your state. Also talk to your family and doctor regarding end-of-life care decisions. Should you be incapacitated, what are your preferences regarding life support, feeding tubes, brain damage, coma, organ and tissue donations, and the like. It's not a pretty topic, but better faced now than later.

"I told my wife to cremate me...she knows what to do."
"My mom knows my wishes - I refuse to be on life support."
"I talk to my kids about this often, so they know my thoughts about feeding tubes."

Sound familiar? Good luck! If your instructions are not **<u>documented</u>** in a proper legal fashion, all kinds of fiascos can ensue. All of a sudden, the state, an ex-spouse, brother, mother-in-law, or you name it decides they know what you would want. Let the drama and the legal battles begin!

No thank you. Don't cause unnecessary heartache and grief for yourself or your loved ones. Show them that you love them. Take the time to get a Living Will; no questions, no ambiguity. Don't wait, get it done!

Power of Attorney (POA).

A POA is a legal document that allows you to appoint a person to manage your affairs if you're unable to do so. You may be incapacitated due to illness or injury. If so, the appointee specified within your POA has the authority that you've granted. There are many different types of POAs and authority to grant, but some of the more common ones are listed below.

General POA - gives broad power to someone over your affairs. This could include financial transactions, employing professional help, settling claims, buying or selling assets, and more. It is often used as part of an estate plan to give an executor the authority to carry out your wishes upon your death.

Special (or Specific) POA - gives very narrow power to someone for a specific function (selling a vehicle, managing property, business transactions, etc). This may allow someone to sell your car or house while you're away on vacation. It may also be used to grant someone power to handle specific financial transactions if you're unable to (pay bills, make transfers, etc).

HealthCare POA - gives someone the authority to make healthcare decisions for you in the event you're unable to speak for yourself. This document can work in conjunction with a Living Will and is generally for unforeseen circumstances. Talk with an attorney.

Trust.

A trust is a legal document that is generally more complex than a Will. I'd argue that by and large, most people do not require a trust. However, there are circumstances where a trust would be valuable. In general, a trust is used to avoid probate, provide privacy or protection of assets from liability, or to minimize estate taxes. Avoiding probate can save thousands of dollars and lots of time. Would you prefer your money go to your heirs and children, or attorneys and probate fees? If any of these situations apply to you, or you have a considerable estate (i.e. $1 Million and up), then consult an estate planning attorney.

Again, this book does not provide legal advice, so be sure to consult a qualified professional. However, estate planning is a very important topic that few people build into their financial house. All too often, they focus only on budgeting and investing. The above items must be considered, and completed, in order to have a financial house of brick. You may not need every single one, that's up to your specific situation, so discuss it with an estate planner. But everyone should have *at least* a Will, a living Will (or equivalent), and associated powers of attorney. You've worked long and hard for what you have, so don't let it be squandered away in taxes, probate fees, and post-funeral bickering about who gets what. Your family deserves better. You also want to be sure someone can speak on your behalf if you become incapacitated. Ok, so once you complete your legal estate plan documents, what do you do with them?

Completing your Will, POAs and other estate plan documents is a major step in your financial success. However, don't just throw these critical documents in a cabinet somewhere and call it a day.

First of all, have two copies of everything. Having more than two copies can cause confusion. If you have only one, it can be lost, stolen, or burned all too easily. Keep your estate plan documents neatly organized in a file folder. I suggest you keep one copy in your house and store another copy at a close relative's house or in a safe deposit box. If you store copies at home, they should be in a fireproof and waterproof safe. You should also keep a separate document that lists your assets. Include things such as bank accounts, mutual funds, real estate records, etc. Be sure to list the address and phone number to your bank. If you own any vehicles, be sure to document where the titles can be found.

Secondly, and probably just as important is to tell someone! Make sure your heirs, executor, and/or family members know that you have these documents, where they are, and how to access them when you die (key, combination, lockbox, password, etc). Your estate plan documents will be meaningless if nobody knows they exist.

Lastly, be sure to keep both copies updated any time you make a change. You want both copies to be identical. If anything requires a notary, ensure you get them re-notarized so they're valid. Then, when all of that is complete, you can sleep soundly at night knowing your family will be well cared for when you die. Speaking of family, it's time to check in on Phil.

Wow, Phil moves fast! Not only did he just buy a house, but he recently got married. He's now a family man. Let's look at his updated biography and budget.

Name:	Phil T. Pig
Age:	25
Marital Status:	Married
Children:	None
Profession:	Electrician
Salary:	$83,040 (combined household)
Retirement Age:	65
Retirement Dream:	Fly Fish & Travel all 50 States
Home Status:	15-yr, 4% fixed rate mortgage

Financial Status:

Financial Component	Status
Income	**Started; Growing**
Budget	**Complete**
Debt	**$0 (debt free)**
Emergency Fund	**Complete**
Retirement	**Started; saving 10% of income**
House	**15-year, 4% fixed rate loan**
Estate Plan	**Complete**
Insurance	Chapter 10
College Fund	Chapter 11

Phil's budget worksheet. Updates in gray and **bold**.

Monthly Pay (take-home)	Jul	Aug	Sep
Job =	$3,360		
Spouse's Job (N/A) =	**$3,560**		
Extra Job/Overtime (N/A) =	$0		
Total Income =	**$6,920**	$0	$0
Monthly Expenses	Jun	Jul	Aug
Entertainment	**$350**		
Eating Out	**$275**		
Miscellaneous	**$60**		
Cable TV	$85		
Cell Phone	**$90**		
Retirement	**$692**		
Discretionary Total =	**$1,552**	$0	$0
Gasoline (avg)	**$400**		
Car Maintenance (avg $420/yr)	**$70**		
Car Insurance	**$150**		
Property Taxes	$100		
Homeowner's Insurance	$90		
Mortgage	$800		
Dental Insurance (family plan)	**$210**		
Health Insurance (family plan)	**$375**		
Electric (avg)	**$190**		
Water (avg)	**$85**		
Gas (avg)	**$90**		
Groceries (avg)	**$550**		
Essential Living Total =	**$3,110**	$0	$0
TOTAL Expenses =	**$4,662**	$0	$0
Excess =	**$2,258**	$0	$0

Budget Breakdown:

- Total Income = $6,920.
- Discretionary Total = $1,552.
- Essential Living Total = $3,110.
- Total Expenses = $4,662.
- Excess = $2,258.
- Debt = $0.
- *Emergency Fund = $18,660 ($3,110 x 6).
- Retirement = $692 (on track; 10% of take-home pay).
- House = 15-yr, 4% fixed rate loan.
- Estate Plan = Complete (Will, Living Will, POAs).
- Insurance = car, rent, dental, health (more in Chapter 10).
- College Fund = No kids (he has one in Chapter 11).
- *Since Phil got married, his essential living expenses have increased. This, in turn, has increased his emergency fund requirement (but it's still 6-months of living expenses).

Notice how Phil updated his budget to incorporate his wife's income. Their expenses went up as well, but with two earners in the household, they can easily afford it. Since Phil and his wife have $2,258 *excess* money every month, this is the time to really start living and also paying down their mortgage very rapidly. Once they eliminate their mortgage, they'll have over $3,000 per month in excess money! Now *that's* rich living! Let's pause here for a moment and look at two items in particular in their budget; retirement and emergency fund.

Since their household income has increased, so too has the 10% requirement for their retirement savings. It went from $336 per month to $692 (10% of $6,920). As stated in Chapter 7, the 10% rule is a just a baseline. Because they've followed the piggy principles, they can afford to really beef up their retirement fund if they choose to do so. They have $2,258 excess every month. Just for fun, if they added a mere $500 of that to the $692 they're already saving, earning 8%, it would grow to over $4 Million in 40 years. They'd truly be living high on the hog! That's the power of compound interest. In addition to their retirement looking pretty bright, they also have a nice cushiony emergency fund.

Since his living expenses increased after getting married, the amount of savings that Phil and his wife need in an emergency fund also increased. Since his wife already had some savings of her own, they simply combined finances to build an appropriate 6-month emergency fund. You might ask yourself why they still need six full months of living expenses since the likelihood of both Phil *and* his wife losing their jobs simultaneously is very low. Yes, you *might* ask that. However, since you're a rich little piggy in training, let me answer that with some questions of my own. Why not live just *partially* debt free? Why not just earn $2,000 per month instead of $3,000 per month? Why pay cash when you can take out a payday loan? I think you get it by now; it's about following the principles and actually *living* them! That's how you get to live like a rich little piggy. However, if you ever get tired of having excess money every month, you can always go back to the "normal" way of doing things. Houses of straw are *easy* to build. Go ahead and spend your emergency fund on a new car and start living off credit cards. No problem, that's easy to do - real easy. But no self-respecting piggy would even think of doing such a thing, so no need to worry about that. So, we've got our finances in order and our estate plan complete. Phil and his wife are protected with the basics in place. Let's see what insurance they might need.

Key Takeaways:
- Everyone should have an estate plan.
- Have at least these minimum documents:
    - Will.
    - Living Will (or equivalent medical directive).
    - Applicable Powers of Attorney.
- Have 2 copies of your estate plan documents.
- Store documents in a fireproof & waterproof safe.
- Discuss your estate plan with your family/heirs.

"Don't go broke trying to look rich. Act your wage."
-Author Unknown

David W. Robbins

CHAPTER 10
INSURANCE (ROOF)

Boom! Your car gets smashed by a drunk driver and now you're hospitalized for 3 weeks. You'll be restricted to bed rest for another 2 weeks, followed by 3 more weeks of rehabilitation and physical therapy. Are you financially prepared? How do you pay your bills? What if you suffered a debilitating injury or illness that jeopardized your job and entire career? The answer to most of these questions is to have insurance.

Insurance is not a foolproof solution to life's surprises, but it can help save you from financial ruin. Insurance forms the roof of your financial house, to shield you from the storms of life; natural disaster, disability, illness, death, accidents, and more. And remember, it's your house's foundation (your budget superpower) that enables you to *adjust your insurance needs*. There are countless types of insurance available out there, but we'll focus on the most common, and most pertinent, to protecting your financial house.

Some insurance is not cheap. Sometimes you can't afford to get it and sometimes you can't afford *not* to get it. By routinely reviewing your budget, you'll be able to see gaps in coverage. All of your insurance expenses should be listed as separate items on your budget. For example, you would not list "mortgage" on your budget and include your homeowners insurance in that same expense. Neither would you list "insurance" as a single expense item, but rather break them all out separately; remember, *categorization*. Realize there's no single rule to follow for insurance, but here are some guidelines for building a sound financial future.

When to get Insurance?

Lots of people ask when they should get insurance. For the most part, it depends on the type of insurance. Buying insurance is not dependent on how much debt you have, whether or not your emergency fund is complete, or if you're currently saving for retirement. Insurance is contingent upon the life situation that you're in. For example, if you don't have a car, you obviously don't need car insurance. If you're in your early 20s and healthy, you probably don't need long-term care insurance. Listed below are the most common types of insurance you'll require throughout your life. We'll find out when you should consider buying each type and how it fits into your financial house.
HealthCare.

When to get it: If you're alive. Before you fall off your parents' healthcare insurance, you must get your own. Get it. Have it. Always.

How it fits in: According to a recent study reported by CNBC news, unpaid medical bills are the number one cause of bankruptcy, with nearly 2 million people affected. Even having coverage won't completely protect you from unpaid medical bills, but imagine if you *don't* have coverage. Lack of healthcare insurance can devastate your finances and leave you with mountains of unpaid medical debt. As stated in Chapter 2, many employers offer healthcare plans that are relatively affordable. Try to find an employer that does. Healthcare benefits should be considered in your overall decision on where to work. If not, healthcare is also available through private, federal and state exchanges. Shop around. Compare premiums, co-pays, and coverage limits. Whether you obtain it from your employer or a federal or state exchange, get healthcare insurance now!

Life.

When to get it: As you know, we all die. If someone relies on your income, you should get life insurance to replace that income when you die. Generally, you need life insurance if you're married, have children, or are someone's caregiver (ailing parent, grandparent, family member, etc).

How it fits in: The idea is to cover your beneficiaries' living expenses and pay off any debt that you're responsible for when you die. How would your family or dependents replace your income? Life insurance is a good solution. How much life insurance should you have? It depends. If you're young and the sole bread winner for a large family and have little in savings, I'd recommend about 20 times your annual salary. So, if you earn $50K/year, you want about $1 Million in *term* life insurance. That may seem like a lot, but if you're healthy, it should cost very little for that coverage. Also, just think about it, $1 Million earning 5% interest is $50K/year (your salary). Sure, you may average more than 5%, but there's a chance you may not; do you want to gamble on your family's future? However, what if you're in your late 50s to early 60s and have zero debt, a paid-off house and $750K in retirement? Well, you would not need life insurance at that point. Your spouse, or other beneficiary, would be more than taken care of and not left with a financial burden. How much life insurance to have is only one consideration.

How long should you have life insurance for? It too, depends. Using the same scenario of a young (late 20s, early 30s) sole bread winner earning $50K/year, you'd want a good **20-year** *term* policy. Those 20 years should provide you enough time to get your kids off to college and build up enough savings to provide your spouse with income if you die during that period. However, if you're in your 50s and have a hefty retirement account built up, you may only need a 10-year policy. It's important to get a level, *term*, fixed premium policy. Do not get whole, variable, universal, or any other "savings/investment" type of insurance. Get simple, *term* coverage with a fixed premium that does not go up or down; for example, $35/month. Your coverage amount should also be a fixed amount; for example, $1 Million. There are links in Appendix C that you can refer to for more information on life insurance and the different types that are available. Basically, whole life policies are a complete waste of money. When you *invest*, do so in good quality, long-term, balanced mutual funds, *not* a life insurance policy. So, it's easy to shop for insurance when you're healthy, but what if you're not?

If you're unhealthy and/or suffering from a major illness or disease, you may not be able to get any life insurance. You must remember this because many single people have blown off getting coverage because they didn't have a spouse or kids (at the time). However, if you're deemed uninsurable a year down the road due to a health condition, you're out of luck. Now, if things change and you get married, have kids, or adopt, it's too late; you're now uninsurable. So, if you even think you *might* have a 'significant other' (beneficiary) in your life, you might consider getting life insurance when you're young, still healthy, and can afford it. The way I look at life insurance is this - as long as I'm healthy, when in doubt, I err on the side of getting "too much" for "too long" since it's so affordable. You can always cancel your policy or change the beneficiary later in life. Speaking of being healthy, there's another type of insurance that you'll need to consider.

Disability.

When to get it: If you're working.

How it fits in: So, life insurance is handy for when you *die*, but what if you're stricken with *illness* or *injury* - you're still alive, but unable to work? Well, say hello to disability insurance! Disability insurance is pretty much what is sounds like. It pays if you become sick or injured and unable to work. You can get short-term and long-term policies as well as coverage for injury only or injury *and* illness. Obviously, the more coverage you get, the higher the premium, but that's something to consider. Some employers offer disability insurance. Try to find one that does. In fact, one of the many benefits of government employment or serving in the military is that you're covered to some degree if you're unable to work due to illness or injury. Unfortunately, it will not last forever and is not a complete solution to a major disability, but it's a starting point. Just like the rest of your financial house, you should build a web, or a layered approach to your finances, and insurance is no different. Try to have a primary plan, in this case, disability insurance, but also be debt free, have savings, minimize living expenses, and grow your retirement. All of these things combined, not just one, will serve you well if you happen to become disabled for a period of time. If your employer does not offer disability insurance, you must shop around. You must weigh the risk and cost of being disabled for any length of time against the cost of the insurance. How will you pay your bills? Do you have debt? See, this is where your good old friend the *Emergency Fund* also comes into play. If you're disabled for a few months, financially speaking, it's "no big deal" if you have a 6-month Emergency Fund. Oh, the love of our financial blueprint. That's precisely why we're building our financial house of *brick*, baby! Even when you have your 6-month emergency fund, I advise you always have disability insurance when you're working. As with any insurance, be sure to research the policy details before purchasing anything. Another type of insurance to consider is long-term care insurance.

Long-Term Care.

When to get it: There's no "right age", but generally, when you're in your mid 50s.

How it fits in: It provides care for people who need help performing every day tasks due to a chronic illness, injury, disability, or the aging process. This care may be required for the rest of your life. It covers expenses for things such as hospice care, nursing homes, and in-home healthcare for life's daily activities (bathing, medication, dressing, etc). The cost of this type of care without insurance can be extremely costly. So, not only do you have your health to worry about, but also your pearly whites.

Dental.

When to get it: If you have teeth.

How it fits in: Arguably not as critical as life or disability insurance, dental insurance can definitely pay off, especially if you have kids. If you're single and have strong, healthy teeth, there's a good chance you'll never encounter a large dental bill. Do you want to take that chance? Do you want to live in a house of straw, *hoping* there's no hurricane?

Even basic cleanings are not cheap nowadays, especially if you have to pay out of your own pocket. I advise, with rare exception, that if you have teeth, you should have dental insurance. In the big picture, it's relatively affordable for offsetting the risk of a huge dental expense. Even one moderately complicated dental problem can cost thousands and thousands of dollars. Be sure to cover yourself and any family members. Once you've got your choppers covered, don't forget your most prized asset - your home.

Homeowners.

When to get it: When you buy a house.

How it fits in: You've worked so long and hard to buy your dream home, so be sure to protect it! Not doing so can cost you dearly. A house is an expensive item, normally the biggest purchase that most people will make in their lifetime. Homeowner's insurance is pretty straight forward, but be sure to read the "fine print". As with any policy, but especially with homeowners, you want to understand your coverage. Seemingly simple things can cost you very high premiums. Things such as trampolines, pools and certain pets can raise your rates significantly. Like most things, they're nice to have, if you can afford them. Also, I've never had a homeowners policy that also covered flood damage. (Many folks don't know that). You want to ask about natural disasters, vandalism, fire, sink holes, and anything else that might be pertinent to your area, for example, heavy snow causing a roof collapse. You should ask what coverage you have if an appliance or a pipe bursts and causes severe water damage. Also understand what coverage you have on the contents of your home. Do you have *replacement* or *cash-value* coverage? Replacement coverage will replace that 60-inch LCD TV, whereas cash-value will give you what it's worth today, after depreciation (used value). These are just some things to consider, so dig deep and understand your policy. Not paying attention can cost you thousands, if not tens of thousands of dollars. The devil is always in the details. Since we mentioned standard homeowner policies do not cover flood damage, is your home in a flood zone?

Flood.

When to get it: If you're house is in a flood zone. You might also consider it if your house is on the edge of a flood zone.

How it fits in: First of all, you should avoid buying a house in a flood zone at all costs. There are too many houses available to choose one that's in a *known* flood area. However, if for some crazy reason, you do decide to buy a house in a flood zone...you should quickly change your mind and not buy it! Ok, kidding aside, maybe you bought a house in a flood zone, or more likely, your existing home is *re-zoned* into one. In this case, your lender will require you to have flood insurance, which can be costly. If your house is paid off (no mortgage), then you will not be *required* to purchase flood insurance. However, a "fool and his money are soon parted" as the saying goes. It would be super unwise to not have flood insurance if your house is zoned in a flood plain. This is not meant to scare you away from buying a house, but rather to inform you so that it can be factored into your finances. Some homes are right on the edge of a flood zone. This means they may not be prone to flooding right now, but could be in the future. Again, do you chance the risk and not get insurance? Be sure to check the flood maps in your area; there are many county, state, and federal maps on the Internet. The Federal Emergency Management Agency is also a good place to start, for both flood zone maps and flood insurance. I've included links in Appendix C also. So, yes, flood zones are a risk. So, flood insurance is another type of insurance to consider, but it's not only for homeowners.

Renters.

When to get it: If you rent your home.

How it fits in: Since renters need insurance too, and we just discussed flood insurance, why not start there? Be sure to check your renter's policy to see if your *belongings* are covered for flood damage. Although you aren't responsible for flood damage to the house or building structure itself, you want to be sure your belongings are covered. Furniture and electronics can be quite expensive to replace. Most of the time, landlords are not good at advising tenants that the property is in or near a flood zone. After all, that would be bad for business. In addition to flood damage, check your policy for contents coverage in general (fire, theft, etc); is it *replacement* or *cash-value* coverage? Also, just like homeowner's insurance, some things can raise your rates significantly (trampolines, certain dogs, etc). So, once your home is covered, don't forget your vehicle.

Vehicle.

When to get it: When you buy a vehicle. This includes cars, trucks, boats, recreation vehicles, motorcycles, etc.

How it fits in: The U.S. Census Bureau reports that from 2004 to 2009, there were over 10 million motor vehicle accidents *each year*. Some accidents are unavoidable, but preventing a huge vehicle repair bill *is* avoidable. You should ensure you have not only adequate coverage on your vehicle, but also coverage for yourself and passengers. Some drivers like to break the law by driving without insurance, so you must protect against them also by having uninsured motorist coverage. Always check your bodily injury limits because some insurance companies will quote bare bones, state minimums in order to quote you a lower premium. Lower premiums are nice, but not at the expense of adequate coverage. What is adequate coverage? Well, can you afford to pay for $10,000 in medial bills? How about $50,000 or $100,000? You must decide what's right for you, but do NOT convince yourself that an accident will not happen, just so you can save a few dollars per month in premiums. When shopping insurance companies' rates, always compare apples to apples in terms of coverage, including deductibles. Now that you have your vehicle insured, here are some ways to lower *all* of your insurance costs.

When it comes to any insurance, you should routinely question whether you're over insured, or under insured. Sometimes you have insurance you don't really need (i.e. smart phone insurance), while other times you don't have insurance that you should. It's difficult and smart to be over-insured, but easy and unwise to be under-insured. One rule to saving money on insurance is to simply shop around. You must compare rates (apples to apples) with at least 3 different companies in order to find the best rates. That means when one company quotes you a lower premium than another company, ensure it's for identical coverage and deductibles.

Additionally, once you settle on a particular company, don't be afraid to shop around in a year or two for an even better rate. Companies are continually striving to be more competitive and balance their risk portfolios, so by shopping competitors, you can save more than you think.

Another way to lower your premium is to raise your deductibles, if you can afford them. For example, the deductible on hurricane damage to your house might be $1,000. If you raise it to $2,000, your premium will be lower. Just do the math to see if it's worth it. If your premium goes down by $250/year, then in 4 years, you'll have saved up that extra $1,000 in a higher deductible. The same for your vehicles; adjust the deductible as high as you can afford to pay, in return for lower premiums. So, these are just a few ways you can save money on your insurance needs, but there are many more. There are entire books devoted solely to understanding and maximizing insurance.

The intent here is to simply show how it fits into building your financial house. Again, insurance is the roof that will shield you from life's storms. Don't let too much of it, or a lack of it, ruin you. Now that you know how to save a few dollars on insurance, let's see how Phil and his spouse are doing.

As you can see in Phil's financial status, he and his wife are now fully covered with applicable insurance.

Financial Status:

Financial Component	Status
Income	Started; Growing
Budget	Complete
Debt	$0 (debt free)
Emergency Fund	Complete
Retirement	Started; saving 10% of income
House	15-year, 4% fixed rate loan
Estate Plan	Complete
Insurance	Fully covered
College Fund	Chapter 11

Looking at Phil's budget, you'll notice how each separate insurance item is categorized on its own. That provides a quick look at how much each policy is costing the couple every month. Since Phil and his wife are relatively young and in good health, their premiums are quite affordable. If they had waited until they were older or ill, they'd be paying much higher rates. That's one more reason you should not delay getting life insurance.

Phil's budget. Updates in gray and **bold**.

Monthly Pay (take-home)	Jul	Aug	Sep
Job =	$3,360	$3,360	
Spouse's Job (N/A) =	$3,560	$3,560	
Extra Job/Overtime (N/A) =	$0	$0	
Total Income =	$6,920	$6,920	$0
Monthly Expenses	Jun	Jun	Jul
Entertainment	$350	$350	
Eating Out	$275	$275	
Miscellaneous	$60	$60	
Cable TV	$85	$85	
Cell Phone	$90	$90	
Retirement	$692	$692	
Discretionary Total =	$1,552	$1,552	$0
Gasoline (avg)	$400	$400	
Car Maintenance (avg $420/yr)	$70	$70	
Car Insurance	$150	$150	
Property Taxes	$100	$100	
Life insurance (Phil; $800k)	$0	**$38**	
Life insurance (Spouse; $800k)	$0	**$35**	
Disability Insurance (both)	$0	**$80**	
Homeowner's Insurance	$90	$90	
Mortgage	$800	$800	
Dental Insurance (family plan)	$210	$210	
Health Insurance (family plan)	$375	$375	
Electric (avg)	$190	$190	
Water (avg)	$85	$85	
Gas (avg)	$90	$90	
Groceries (avg)	$550	$550	
Essential Living Total =	$3,110	**$3,263**	$0
TOTAL Expenses =	$4,662	**$4,815**	$0
Excess =	$2,258	**$2,105**	$0

Budget Breakdown:

- Total Income = $6,920.
- Discretionary Total = $1,552.
- Essential Living Total = $3,263.
- Total Expenses = $4,815.
- Excess = $2,105.
- Debt = $0.
- Emergency Fund = $19,578 ($3,263 x 6).
- Retirement = $692 (on track; 10% of take-home pay).
- House = 15-yr, 4% fixed rate loan.
- Estate Plan = Complete (Will, Living Will, POAs).
- Insurance = car, rent, dental, health, life and disability.
- College Fund = No kids (he has one in Chapter 11).
- Phil and his wife each bought $800K life insurance policies (about 20 times their income). They also bought disability insurance through their employers.

Since Phil and his wife are both fairly young, they each took out a 20-year level, term life insurance policy. Each policy is $800,000, which is a little less than 20 times their annual salary. Sadly, there are too many couples out there with either too little life insurance, or none at all. What a catastrophe waiting to happen! As inexpensive as it is, life insurance provides a HUGE safety net to your financial health. Imagine Phil or his wife were to pass away within the next 20 years; how would that affect their finances? The survivor would be devastated emotionally, but then they'd be kicked while they're down because their income just got cut in half! Luckily, Phil's a smart little guy, so in addition to life insurance, he and his wife also purchased disability insurance.

Disability insurance will cover Phil and his wife in the event they become ill or injured and unable to work. By setting up the proper insurance, Phil and his wife are now protected from life's nasty storms. So, that's your financial house, from bottom to top. But did we forget anything?

Key Takeaways:
- Purchase insurance contingent upon your life situation.
- When buying life insurance, always buy a term policy.
- When buying any insurance, always shop around.
- If you can afford it, lower premiums by raising deductibles.

"If you don't want to work, you have to work to earn enough money so that you won't have to work." -Ogden Nash

David W. Robbins

CHAPTER 11
HEY, WAIT A MINUTE! (COLLEGE FUND)

Congratulations, you've finished building your financial house of brick! But hey, wait a minute...what about my kid's college fund?! Well, the blueprint you just followed was for *everyone* to use. However, if you have children, there's one last piece of the puzzle. A college fund is not really a part of your financial house, but it *is* a financial link, connecting one generation to the next. That's why a college fund is not one of the piggy principles. The piggy principles apply to everyone, and obviously not everyone has kids. It's important to help your kids get started in college. However, as critical as it may be to *their* financial house, it is not critical to *your* financial house. After all, why not fund their retirement account, or buy them a house while you're at it? Well, those are hurtful hand *outs*. You want to provide helpful hand *ups*! You must draw the line somewhere between dependent childhood and independent adulthood; piggy philosophy draws it here. This is not to be mean to your kids, so allow me to explain. If you've ever taken an airplane flight, you'll remember when the flight attendant briefs the passengers on how to use their oxygen mask. They tell you to put yours on first before trying to put on your child's oxygen mask. This is for, hopefully, obvious reasons. If you get light-headed and pass out first, you will not be able to tend to either yourself or your child's needs. So, you always put on your oxygen mask first and then help your child put on theirs. You should follow the same approach when building your financial house. Once yours is complete, you are then able to help your children to start building their financial house. Then, when they leave the nest, set them up for success by handing them a copy of this book! So, where does a college fund fall in the priority of your budget?

Unfortunately, too many parents have their heart in the right place, but not necessarily their head when it comes to their finances and their children. You've heard the stories of parents saving like crazy for their kids' college fund, yet they have a mountain of debt, no savings, and are not putting one dime towards their own retirement. This is a catastrophe waiting to happen. With some luck, the child will go to college, only to end up supporting their own parents during what should be their parents' golden years. They'll both end up struggling financially, starting the cycle all over again. Not in *this* brick house! Let's look at our pay priority to see where a college fund falls.

Pay **Last** --> #7 - Disposable (play money)
             #6 - College Fund (if applicable)
             #5 - Mortgage (if applicable)
             #4 - Retirement (10% of take-home pay)
             #3 - Emergency Fund (6-months of expenses)
             #2 - Debt (100% debt-free, except house)
Pay **First** --> #1 - Essential Living Expenses

As you can see, a college fund falls at #6; it comes *after* buying a house (if you choose to buy one), but *before* spending all of your disposable "play money". This implies that everything from #1 to #5 should be paid *before* a college fund. That means your essential living expenses are first, then pay off all debt and build your 6-month emergency fund. Once that's complete, start saving 10% of your income for retirement and if you choose to do so, buy a house. If you don't buy a house, then simply start building your college fund once you're saving 10% for retirement every month. Any money left over after your monthly retirement savings and mortgage payments can go towards building a college fund. Let's see how that works.

So, if you have children, let's examine *how* to build their college fund. After all, pre-funding is a method we can use to give our children a financial hand up in today's world. As you'll recall, *pre-funding* is one of the strategies we use for avoiding debt (Chapter 5). What better way to avoid debt, than to avoid mountains of student loans. Sadly, the complexity of college savings plans can make your head spin. Truly understanding the specifics of each program will take some research. For the most part, there are three main "categories" of college savings plans (aka college funds): **Coverdell Education Savings Account (ESA)**, the **529 Plan** (named after the IRS code that authorizes it), and **Pre-paid Tuition Plans**. Let's take a high-level look at each and a possible alternative to these complex solutions. After all, piggies like to keep things simple.

Coverdell ESA.

The ESA is a tax-deferred account that can be used to fund educational expenses for beneficiaries 18 years old or younger. Contributions can be invested in assets such as stocks, bonds, mutual funds, and certificates of deposit. The maximum contribution limit is $2,000 per year, per child. Funds withdrawn may be tax-free, when used for qualified education expenses. Any balance in the ESA must be used or transferred to another eligible family member when the beneficiary reaches age 30 or dies.

529 Plan.

The 529 Plan is a state-sponsored plan. This is a tax-deferred account that can be used to fund educational expenses for beneficiaries of any age. There are two main types within 529 plans: *pre-paid tuition* and *savings*. *Pre-paid tuition* pays for future tuition at today's rate. This is supposed to protect against inflation and skyrocketing tuition costs. The *savings plan* allows you invest in assets such as stocks, bonds, mutual funds, and certificates of deposit, allowing your contributions grow tax-deferred to pay for future tuition. The maximum contributions are much higher than ESA plans. Funds withdrawn may be tax-free, when used for qualified education expenses.

Pre-paid Tuition Plan.

The pre-paid tuition plans are generally state-sponsored. In short, they allow parents or other sponsor to essentially buy, or pre-pay, future tuition at today's rate. There are many stipulations and requirements, depending on the state, so contact your state sponsor, if you have one; not all states may offer these plans. For example, the state of Florida offers a pre-paid plan and one of its benefits is that it's guaranteed by the state; it does not fluctuate with the markets like a 529 plan might. There are also residency requirements with pre-paid tuition plans, so be sure to research your specific state.

Keep in mind, the specifics of the above plans vary greatly, depending on many factors, including state residency, household income levels, tax consequences, and more. Research each carefully before deciding which is best for your situation. The best recommendations is to consult a certified tax professional or financial planner. Some helpful links are included in Appendix C. Although these college savings plan can offer wonderful tax advantages, you usually require at least 10 years of growth in order to ride out fluctuations in the market. If your child is already getting up in age, these plans may be more trouble than they're worth. Do your research and talk with a financial planner. If you're still uncomfortable making an investment into one of the above plans, go the "old school" route.

To avoid doing nothing because of the complexity around college savings plans, you can always just throw money into a mutual fund or a savings account. If you have at least 10 years to account for market fluctuation, you can go with a reputable growth stock mutual fund. By reputable, I mean one that has a proven track record and has been around for *at least* 10 years. However, if you're getting a late start on your child's college fund, simply pile money into a savings account or a certificate of deposit. The downside is that you'll earn very little on your investment, but at least you know for a fact it will be there when you need it. You'll also lose the advantage of tax-deferred or tax-free growth. So be it. Getting it DONE is more important than investing a bunch of money into something you're not comfortable with or has the potential to drop in value right when your child needs it. While saving for your child's college fund is important, don't forget some other options.

Many people don't bother doing their homework when it comes to helping their children pay for college. In addition to a college savings fund, be sure to research opportunities for scholarships and grants. There are many scholarship programs available to help partially, or even completely cover college tuition. Some are academic in nature and others are sports related. Some are publicly funded and others are privately funded. Do your research. Start by contacting the college's admissions office. Some colleges even have an office dedicated to helping students find financial aid resources. Search the Internet for scholarships and grants. You'd be surprised at how much money is available. Leave no stone unturned when it comes to financial aid. The links in Appendix C may also help.

So, we're ready to start our child's college fund, but let's check in one last time with Phil and his wife to see how they're doing.

Uh-oh! Congratulations are in order; Phil and his wife are proud parents of a wee little one. They finally had a child and decided it's time to start saving for college tuition.

Name:	Phil T. Pig
Age:	25
Marital Status:	Married
Children:	One
Profession:	Electrician
Salary:	$83,040 (combined household)
Retirement Age:	65
Retirement Dream:	Fly Fish & Travel all 50 States
Home Status:	15-yr, 4% fixed rate mortgage

Financial Status:

Financial Component	Status
Income	Started; Growing
Budget	Complete
Debt	$0 (debt free)
Emergency Fund	Complete
Retirement	Started; saving 10% of income
House	15-year, 4% fixed rate loan
Estate Plan	Complete
Insurance	Fully covered
College Fund	Started; saving $150 per month

Phil's budget worksheet. Updates in gray and **bold**.

Monthly Pay (take-home)	Jul	Aug	Sep
Job =	$3,360	$3,360	$3,360
Spouse's Job (N/A) =	$3,560	$3,560	$3,560
Extra Job/Overtime (N/A) =	$0	$0	$0
Total Income =	$6,920	$6,920	$6,920
Monthly Expenses	Jun	Jun	Jun
Entertainment	$350	$350	$350
Eating Out	$275	$275	$275
Miscellaneous	$60	$60	$60
Cable TV	$85	$85	$85
Cell Phone	$90	$90	$90
College Fund	$0	$0	**$150**
Retirement	$692	$692	$692
Discretionary Total =	$1,552	$1,552	**$1,702**
Gasoline (avg)	$400	$400	$400
Car Maintenance (avg $420/yr)	$70	$70	$70
Car Insurance	$150	$150	$150
Property Taxes	$100	$100	$100
Life insurance (Phil; $800k)	$0	$38	$38
Life insurance (Spouse; $800k)	$0	$35	$35
Disability Insurance (both)	$0	$80	$80
Homeowner's Insurance	$90	$90	$90
Mortgage	$800	$800	$800
Dental Insurance (family plan)	$210	$210	$210
Health Insurance (family plan)	$375	$375	$375
Electric (avg)	$190	$190	$190
Water (avg)	$85	$85	$85
Gas (avg)	$90	$90	$90
Groceries (avg)	$550	$550	$550
Essential Living Total =	$3,110	$3,263	$3,263
TOTAL Expenses =	$4,662	$4,815	**$4,965**
Excess =	$2,258	$2,105	**$1,955**

Budget Breakdown:

- Total Income = $6,920.
- Discretionary Total = $1,702.
- Essential Living Total = $3,263.
- Total Expenses = $4,965.
- Excess = $1,955.
- Debt = $0.
- Emergency Fund = $19,578 ($3,263 x 6).
- Retirement = $692 (on track; 10% of take-home pay).
- House = 15-yr, 4% fixed rate loan.
- Estate Plan = Complete (Will, Living Will, POAs).
- Insurance = car, rent, dental, health, life and disability.
- College Fund = On track. Saving $150/month. Estimated $72,000 at 8% growth after 18 years.

Phil and his wife decided to save $150 per month in a non-retirement growth mutual fund. They didn't want to deal with the hassle of a 529 Plan or an ESA. If they earn 8% for 18 years, after fees and taxes, they'll have about $72,000 saved for their child's college tuition. Even if they earn HALF that growth (4%), they'll still have about $48,000. Predicting exactly how much college will cost is almost impossible. Phil may save too much, or too little.

As time gets closer to Phil's child approaching college, he can do a much better job predicting tuition costs. He'll also know exactly how much he has saved. If it looks like he'll need more, he can always find ways to add a few hundred more dollars per month into college savings. Additionally, he can always cash flow tuition as their child works his way through school. Many times scholarships and grants are available, in which case Phil and his wife may have money left over. In that event, they can use the extra money to take an exotic vacation! Either way, they'll be just fine because they budgeted accordingly. So there you have it, the last financial link for your financial house.

Key Takeaways:
- Start your child's college fund *after* you:
    - Create your budget.
    - Become debt free.
    - Build a 6-month emergency fund.
    - Start saving 10% of income for retirement
    - Buy a house (if you choose to buy one)
- The 3 main categories of college savings plans are:
    - Coverdell ESA
    - 529 Plan
    - Pre-paid tuition plan
- If all else fails, simply save/invest for college tuition.
- Do your homework and research all financial aid options.

"If you want something you've never had, you must be willing to do something you've never done." -Thomas Jefferson

David W. Robbins

CHAPTER 12
SUMMARY (PARTING PIGGY THOUGHTS)

We started off by asking what it means to be rich. It's not about having millions of dollars, private jets, or a huge mansion. Being rich means having freedom. It's having the freedom to do what you want, when, where, and how you want to do it. Being rich allows you to step off the hamster wheel and travel your own path in life. You spend more time with family and friends and less time working and laboring. It's a feeling of security, comfort and relaxation that comes with knowing your financial house is in order. You know that being rich does not come easy, but you now know the way.

Being rich starts with a sound philosophy - one that is based on *values*. Values such as stoicism, passion, excellence, humility and generosity that will drive your everyday actions. These five core values will guide you when times are tough and ground you when times are good. However, simply having values is not enough. By acting on those values and following a financial blueprint, you must begin to build your financial house. In the first stage, you will focus on building your career, in order to generate income. Never settling for status quo, you'll grow your income through added responsibility, advanced skills training, professional certifications, college education, and remaining mobile. In the second stage, your income will be used to fund your financial house; not a house of straw, but a house of BRICK! You will focus your financial efforts and live a life of cash, not credit. First, you'll follow a written budget, always keeping your total income higher than your total expenses. Then, you'll make sure you get out of debt and stay out of debt, paying cash for everything. Live below your means. Next, you'll build your 6-month emergency fund to help cushion you against life's surprises. Then, you begin saving 10% of your income for retirement. If done correctly, you'll retire a millionaire. Additionally, if and when the time is right, you'll buy the house of your dreams. Your house will be a delight rather than a disaster. Your estate plan will be in order and you'll sleep soundly at night, knowing your insurance umbrella is protecting you from life's nasty storms.

Regardless of where you are in building your financial house, remember the example of Phil T. Pig. He started out with a financial mess. He had credit card debt, car loan debt, and was saving almost nothing for retirement. He was spending excessively on frivolous items while he had no disability insurance or life insurance. Phil had no emergency fund to cushion him against life's surprises. By following the piggy principles, Phil ended up debt-free with a 6-month emergency fund. He's now saving 10% of his income for retirement and is on track to retire a millionaire at age 65. He owns the house of his dreams. Finally, Phil got married and had a kid. He finished things off by getting the disability and life insurance that he needed and started a college fund for his child. Phil and his wife have an excess of about $2,000 per month. Phil is an example of how it can be done. In fact, with their combined incomes, Phil and his wife will most likely retire with far more than a million dollars, and far earlier than age 65. They're the shining example of how to achieve financial success. Having built a financial house, it's time to focus on the last piggy principle.

Piggy principles 1 through 5 have led us to this point, but the real fun begins with principle #6.

1. Grow your income
2. Follow a written budget
3. Live debt free
4. Build a 6-month emergency fund
5. Save 10% of income for retirement
6. **Pay it forward**

Once you've built your financial house, don't stop there. Remember to pay it forward and lend a hand up to those around you. Teach, mentor, coach, and help others; they too, may wish to leave the hamster wheel. You can enlist your friends and family to join the movement. Encourage them to minimize living expenses and live debt free. Show them how an emergency fund can help take the stress out of their life. Let them know they can retire with dignity. Inspire them through your example. Living on credit is not a necessity. There are endless ways to pay it forward. Be creative and have fun with it.

In closing, remember this - this book will do nothing for you if you don't *act* on it. Follow it. Do it. Champion the Piggy Philosophy. Break the traditional mold of run, run, run and go, go, go. Step off the hamster wheel. Quit living paycheck to paycheck. Live life on your terms. Work hard, play harder! Follow the action items in **Appendix A** starting right now. Join the movement - become a Rich Little Piggy!

"If you aim at nothing, you'll hit it every time." -Zig Ziglar

APPENDIX A
ACTION ITEMS

Join the Movement - Become a Piggy!

Check item off when complete.

<u>Like</u> & <u>Share</u> Piggy Facebook Pages:
- ☐ Rich Little Piggy
  Facebook.com/richlittlepiggy
- ☐ Live Debt Free
  Facebook.com/crushdebt
☐ Follow on Twitter @RichLittlePiggy
☐ Share your success stories on piggy pages above.
☐ Mark your calendar (Jan 8th) - celebrate Debt Free Day!

APPENDIX B
PIGGY PHILOSOPHY

Piggy Motto: Work Hard, Play Harder!

Piggy Values (live these):
- Stoicism
- Passion
- Excellence
- Humility
- Generosity

Build Your Career (through these):
- Added Responsibility
- Advanced Skills Training
- Industry Certifications
- College Education
- Mobility

Piggy Principles (do these, in this order):
1. Grow your income
2. Follow a written budget
3. Live debt free
4. Build a 6-month emergency fund
5. Save 10% of income for retirement
6. Pay it forward

Debt Don'ts (heed these):
- NEVER co-sign a loan for ANYONE!
- NEVER take out a payday or title loan!
- NEVER use an unsecured credit card!
- NEVER borrow from your retirement!

Your Budget's 6 Superpowers enable you to:
- Eliminate your **debt**.
- Build your **emergency fund**.
- Fund your **retirement**.
- Afford your **house**.
- Manage your **estate plan**.
- Adjust your **insurance** needs

Piggy Truisms (believe these):
- #1 money problem is **no budget**.
  - Have one & follow it!
- #2 money problem is **too little income**.
  - Always grow your income!

<u>Pay Priority</u>:

Pay **Last** -->   #7 - Disposable (play money)
                  #6 - College Fund (if applicable)
                  #5 - Mortgage (if applicable)
                  #4 - Retirement (10% of take-home pay)
                  #3 - Emergency Fund (6-months of expenses)
                  #2 - Debt (100% debt-free, except house)
Pay **First** -->   #1 - Essential Living Expenses

David W. Robbins

APPENDIX C
USEFUL & COOL PIGGY LINKS

The below links are a mere sampling of my favorites. I've personally used many of these sites while building my career and financial house. Use them as a starting point, but be sure to search out others that pertain to your interests.

Note: Sites subject to change.

Rich Little Piggy

Facebook (Rich Little Piggy)
www.facebook.com/richlittlepiggy

Facebook (Live Debt Free)
www.facebook.com/crushdebt

Twitter: @RichLittlePiggy

Popular Personal Finance Experts

Dave Ramsey
www.daveramsey.com

Suze Orman
www.suzeorman.com

Clark Howard
www.clarkhoward.com

Career Resources

Federal Jobs Portal
www.usajobs.gov

LinkedIn Professional Network
www.linkedin.com

Monster Jobs Board
www.monster.com

CareerBuilder Jobs Board
www.careerbuider.com

Join the Military
http://www.military.com/join-armed-forces

Entrepreneur
www.entrepreneur.com

Professional Certification Organizations

Project Management Institute
www.pmi.org

ISC2
www.isc2.org

CompTIA
www.comptia.org

Lean Six Sigma
www.iassc.org

SME
www.sme.org

Educational Resources

Financial Aid (FAFSA)
www.fafsa.ed.gov

Financial Aid (FINAID)
www.finaid.org

College Savings Plans Network
http://www.collegesavings.org/index.aspx

SavingForCollege.com
http://www.savingforcollege.com/

Financial Resources

Social Security Administration
www.ssa.gov

Thrift Savings Plan
www.tsp.gov

MoneyRates
www.money-rates.com

BankRate
www.bankrate.com

National Foundation for Credit Counseling
www.nfcc.org

Assoc of Independent Consumer Credit Counseling Agencies
www.aiccca.org

Fidelity
www.fidelity.com

Vanguard
www.vanguard.com

Charles Schwab
www.schwab.com

CNN Money Essentials
http://money.cnn.com/magazines/moneymag/money101/

FDIC Bank Find
http://research.fdic.gov/bankfind/

National Credit Union Association
www.ncua.gov

myFICO
www.myfico.com

Annual Credit Reports
www.annualcreditreport.com

Credit Karma
www.creditkarma.com

NAPFA (Financial Advisors)
www.napfa.org

Reference Sites

Life Happens
www.lifehappens.org

Federal Emergency Management Agency
www.fema.gov

Dave Ramsey's Endorsed Local Providers
http://www.daveramsey.com/elp

HealthCare Resources

American Association for Long-Term Care Insurance
http://www.aaltci.org/

LongTermCare.gov
http://longtermcare.gov/

Federal Long Term Care Insurance Program
https://www.ltcfeds.com/

Cool Sites

Mr. Money Mustache
http://www.mrmoneymustache.com/

Retire By 40
http://retireby40.org/

ABOUT THE AUTHOR

Dave comes from loving but humble beginnings. He enlisted in the U.S. Air Force in 1988 - his base pay was $630.70 per month. As a communications specialist, he worked in many world-wide locations, serving with the finest professionals in the world. After retiring from service in 2010, he worked for about 4 years as an Information Technology Specialist for the Department of the Air Force and the Department of the Treasury. Over his career, he earned a Masters of Science Degree in Management from Troy University and 6 professional certifications, including Project Management Professional and Certified Information Systems Security Professional. However, the crowning achievement of his life has been his wonderful family. Dave married his beautiful wife Judette in 2004 and together, they've been raising the best two children that parents could ask for. However, with a severely ill family member he took a hiatus from his career, resigning from a rewarding and lucrative position. This ultimately led to his decision to retire from work permanently - at the age of 43, he was done. Spending time with family and friends and enjoying the richness of life is a rare commodity. Dave does not take it for granted and believes the ability to choose family over work is achievable by all. His fortunate blessing was enabled by a career path, educational studies, and ultimately by a life philosophy that Dave has documented in his book "Rich Little Piggy". In the spirit of paying it forward, his mission is helping everyday people achieve financial success - please join him!

Made in the USA
San Bernardino, CA
10 February 2015